STRING THEORY

STRING
THE◯RY

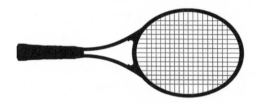

DAVID FOSTER
WALLACE
ON TENNIS

INTRODUCTION BY
JOHN JEREMIAH SULLIVAN

A Library of America Special Publication

Visit our website at www.loa.org.

Published by arrangement with Little, Brown and Company,
New York, N.Y. All rights reserved.

The list of sources and acknowledgments constitutes
an extension of this copyright page.
Endpaper image courtesy of iStock.com/Pavlo_K.

This paper meets the requirements of
ANSI/NISO Z39.48–1992 (Permanence of Paper).

Distributed to the trade in the United States
by Penguin Random House Inc.
and in Canada by Penguin Random House Canada Ltd.

Library of Congress Control Number: 2015951697
ISBN 978–1–59853–480–1

Third Printing

Manufactured in the United States of America

Contents

Introduction
by John Jeremiah Sullivan

"TENNIS" IS A wonderful word in the sense that it never really existed. That is, although the game is French to the core—not one but two of France's early kings died at the tennis courts, and the Republic was born on one, with the Tennis Court Oath—the French never called it that, tennis. They called it *Jeu de paume*, the "game of the palm," or "handball" if we want to be less awkwardly literal about it (originally they had played it with the bare hand, then came gloves, then paddles, then rackets). When the French would go to serve, they often said *Tenez!*, the French word for "take it," meaning "coming at you, heads up." We preserve this custom of warning the opponent in our less lyrical way by stating the score just before we toss up the ball. It was the Italians who, having overheard the French make these sounds, began calling the game "ten-ez" by association. A lovely detail in that it suggests a scene, a Florentine ear at the fence or the entryway, listening. They often built those early courts in the forest, in clearings. The call in the air. Easy to think of Benjy in *The Sound and the Fury*, hearing the golfers shout "Caddy!" and assuming they mean his sister, only here the word moves between languages, out of France via the transnational culture of the aristocratic court and into Italy. There it enters European literature around the 1350s, the time of Petrarch's *Phisicke Against Fortune*. In considering the anxiety that consumes so much of human experience, he writes, "And what is the cause hereof, but only our own lightness & daintiness: for we seem to be good for nothing else, but to be tossed hither & thither like a Tennise bal, being creatures of very short life, of infinite care-fulness, & yet ignorant unto what shore to sail with our ship . . ."

A metaphor for human existence, then, and for fate: "We are merely the stars' tennis-balls," in John Webster's *Duchess of Malfi*, "struck and banded / Which way please them." That is one tradition. In another, tennis becomes a symbol of frivolity, of a different kind of "lightness." Grown men playing with balls. The history of the game's being used that way is twined up with an anecdote from the reign of Henry V, the powerful young king who had once been Shakespeare's reckless Prince Hal. According to one early chronicler, "the Dauphin, thinking King Henry to be given to such plays and light follies . . . sent to him a tun of tennis-balls." King Henry's imagined reply at the battle of Agincourt was rendered into verse, probably by the poet-monk John Lydgate, around 1536:

> Some hard tennis balls I have hither brought
> Of marble and iron made full round.
> I swear, by Jesu that me dear bought,
> They shall beat the walls to the ground.

That story flowers into a couplet of Shakespeare's *Henry V*, ca. 1599. The package from the Dauphin arrives. Henry's uncle, the Duke of Exeter, takes it. "What treasure, uncle?" asks the king. "Tennis-balls, my liege," Exeter answers. "And we understand him well," Henry says (a line meant to echo an earlier one, said under very different circumstances, Hal's equally famous "I know you all and will awhile uphold"):

> How he comes o'er us with our wilder days
> Not measuring what use we made of them.

A more eccentric instance of tennis-as-metaphor pops up in Shakespeare's *Pericles*, where the tennis court is compared with the ocean. It occurs in the part of the play that scholars now believe was written by a tavern-keeper named George Wilkins. Pericles has just been tossed half dead onto the Greek shore and is discovered by three fishermen. He speaks,

> A man whom both the waters and the wind,
> In that vast tennis-court, hath made the ball
> For them to play upon, entreats you pity him

. . . lines that may cause some modern readers to recall David Foster Wallace's "Derivative Sport in Tornado Alley," an essay about learning to play the game in the central Midwest, where extreme winds are an almost constant factor, but where Wallace succeeded, he tells us, in part because of a "weird robotic detachment" from the "unfairnesses of wind and weather."

David Foster Wallace wrote about tennis because life gave it to him—he had played the game well at the junior level—and because he was a writer who in his own way made use of wilder days, turning relentlessly in his work to the stuff of his own experience. But the fact of the game in his biography came before any thought of its use as material. At least I assume that's the case. It can be amazing how early in life some writers figure out what they are and start to see their lives as stories that can be controlled. It is perhaps not farfetched to imagine Wallace's noticing early on that tennis is a good sport for literary types and purposes. It draws the obsessive and brooding. It is perhaps the most isolating of games. Even boxers have a corner, but in professional tennis it is a rules violation for your coach to communicate with you beyond polite encouragement, and spectators are asked to keep silent while you play. Your opponent is far away, or if near is indifferently hostile. It may be as close as we come to physical chess, or a kind of chess in which the mind and body are at one in attacking essentially mathematical problems. So, a good game not just for writers but for philosophers too. The perfect game for Wallace.

He wrote about it in fiction, essays, journalism, and reviews. It may be his most consistent theme at the surface level, which is why this collection makes sense. Wallace himself drew attention, consciously or not, to both his love for the game and its relevance to how he saw the world. He knew something, too, about the contemporary literature of the sport. The close attention to both physics and physical detail that energizes the opening of his 1996 *Esquire* piece on a then-young Michael Joyce (a promising power-baseliner who became a sought-after coach and helped Maria Sharapova win two of her Grand Slam titles) echoes clearly the first lines of John McPhee's *Levels of the Game* (one of the few tennis books I can think of that give as much pleasure as the one you're holding): "Arthur Ashe, his feet apart, his knees slightly bent, lifts a tennis ball into the air. The toss is high and forward. If the ball were allowed to drop, it would, in Ashe's words, 'make a parabola . . .'"

For me, the effect of gathering Wallace's tennis-themed nonfiction under one cover is a bit like assembling a mirror, one of those segmented mirrors they build and position in space, only this one is pointed at a writer's mind. The game he writes about is one that, like language, emphasizes the closed system, makes a fetish of it ("Out!"). He seems both to exult and to be trapped in its rules, its cruelties. He loves the game but yearns to transcend it. As always in Wallace's writing Wittgenstein is the philosopher who most haunts the approach, the Wittgenstein who told us that reality is inseparable from language ("The limits of my language mean the limits of my world"), and that language is inseparable from game (both being at root "part of an activity, a form of life").

From such a description a reader might conclude that the writer under discussion was dry and abstract, and in the end only using the sport, in a convenient, manipulative way, to say other things, which he deemed more significant—but that is not the writer you'll meet in the following pages. This is instead one who can transpose on-court sensations into his prose. In those paragraphs that describe how growing up in a windy country shaped his game, briefly allowing him to excel over more talented opponents who tended to get frustrated in unpredictable conditions, he tells us that he was "able to use the currents kind of the way a pitcher uses spit. I could hit curves way out into cross-breezes that'd drop the ball just fair; I had a special wind-serve that had so much spin the ball turned oval in the air and curved left to right . . ." In reviewing Tracy Austin's autobiography, he finds a way, despite his disappointment with the book, to say something about athletic greatness and mediocrity, and what truly differentiates them, remembering how as a player he would often "get divided, paralyzed. As most ungreat athletes do. Freeze up, choke. Lose our focus. Become self-conscious. Cease to be wholly present in our wills and choices and movements." Unlike the great, who become so in part because it would never occur to them not to be "totally present." Their "blindness and dumbness," in other words, are not "the price of the gift" but "its essence," and are even the gift itself. The writer, existing only in reflection, is of all beings most excluded from the highest realms.

Possibly Wallace's finest tennis piece, certainly his most famous, is "Federer Both Flesh and Not," an essay first published in 2006 in the *New York Times'* short-lived sports magazine *Play*. The greatest tennis writer of his generation was writing about the greatest player of his generation. The sentence needs no qualifiers. Federer himself later remarked, in a question-and-answer forum, that he was astonished at what a "comprehensive" piece Wallace had produced, despite the fact that the writer had spent only "20 min with him in the ATP office." But I doubt Wallace wanted more face time than that. He had come to Wimbledon in search of not the man Roger Federer but rather the being Federer seemed to become when he competed. What Wallace wanted to see occurred only as spectacle. In that respect and others it is interesting to compare the Federer piece with the profile Wallace had written precisely a decade before, about Michael Joyce. I tend to prefer the earlier piece, for its thick description and subtleties, while recognizing the greatness of the later one. In the Joyce piece, Wallace had written about a nobody, a player no one had heard of and who was never going to make it on the tour. That was the subtext, and at times the text, of the essay: you could be *that* good and still not be good enough. The essay was about agony. In Federer, though, he had a player who offered him a different subject: transcendence. What it actually looked like. An athlete who appeared "to be exempt, at least in part, from certain physical laws." One can see exactly what Wallace means in footage of the point he breaks down so beautifully—a "sixteen-stroke point" that reads as dramatically as a battle scene—which occurred in the second set of Federer's 2006 Wimbledon final match against Rafael Nadal, a point that ends with a backhand one can replay infinite times and somehow come no closer to comprehending, struck from about an inch inside the baseline with some kind of demented spin that causes the ball to *slip* over the net and vanish. Nadal never touches it. Wallace is able not only to give us the moment, but to let us see the strategic and geometric intelligence that went into setting it up, the ability Federer had (has, as of this writing) to "hypnotize" opponents through shot-selection.

The key sentences in the Federer essay, to my mind, occur in the paragraph that mentions "evolution." In discussing the "power-baseline" style that has defined the game in the modern era—two heavy hitters standing back and blasting wrist-fracturing groundstrokes at each other—Wallace writes that "it is not, as pundits have publicly feared for years, the evolutionary endpoint of tennis. The player who's shown this to be true is Roger Federer." One imagines his writing this sentence with something almost like gratitude. It had taken genius to break through the brutal dictates of the power game and bring back an all-court style, to bring back art. And Federer, as Wallace emphasizes, did this from "within" the power game, he did it while handling shots that were moving at hurricane force. Inside the wind tunnel of modern tennis, he crafted a style that seemed made for a butterfly, yet was crushingly effective. What a marvelous subject, and figure, for a twenty-first-century novelist, a writer working in a form that is also (perpetually?) said to be at the end of its evolution, and an artist who similarly, when at his best, showed new ways forward.

By way of ending—or rather of stepping aside—I include a small item from the Champaign-Urbana *News-Gazette*, the daily in the part of Illinois where Wallace played most of his tennis. All players know how much is required both to excel and to remain well regarded among one's peers on the court, where character is often revealed in harsh X-ray. Given that, these three short paragraphs say much, and deserve to be entered into the database of Wallaceiana.

> Not too long after David Foster Wallace committed suicide in 2008, some of his Urbana High School tennis teammates decided to pay tribute to the writer right here in his hometown.
>
> Because Wallace had been a standout tennis player, Rick Goldwasser and others who had competed alongside him decided Blair Park was as good a place as any for a memorial—a plaque or perhaps having the tennis courts named in his honor.
>
> "He was very passionate about tennis, and that's where he played and was in charge of tennis lessons" over two summers, said Goldwasser, who is leading the effort.

—From the Urbana High School Rosemary, *1980, Wallace's senior year. He is standing third from left.*

Derivative Sport
in Tornado Alley

WHEN I LEFT my boxed township of Illinois farmland to attend my dad's alma mater in the lurid jutting Berkshires of western Massachusetts, I all of a sudden developed a jones for mathematics. I'm starting to see why this was so. College math evokes and catharts a Midwesterner's sickness for home. I'd grown up inside vectors, lines and lines athwart lines, grids—and, on the scale of horizons, broad curving lines of geographic force, the weird topographical drain-swirl of a whole lot of ice-ironed land that sits and spins atop plates. The area behind and below these broad curves at the seam of land and sky I could plot by eye way before I came to know infinitesimals as easements, an integral as schema. Math at a hilly Eastern school was like waking up; it dismantled memory and put it in light. Calculus was, quite literally, child's play.

In late childhood I learned how to play tennis on the blacktop courts of a small public park carved from farmland that had been nitrogenized too often to farm anymore. This was in my home of Philo, Illinois, a tiny collection of corn silos and war-era Levittown homes whose native residents did little but sell crop insurance and nitrogen fertilizer and herbicide and collect property taxes from the young academics at nearby Champaign-Urbana's university, whose ranks swelled enough in the flush 1960s to make outlying non sequiturs like "farm and bedroom community" lucid.

Between the ages of twelve and fifteen I was a near-great junior tennis player. I made my competitive bones beating up on lawyers' and dentists' kids at little Champaign and Urbana Country Club events and was soon killing whole summers being driven through dawns to tournaments all over Illinois, Indiana, Iowa. At fourteen I was ranked 17th in the United States Tennis Association's Western Section ("Western" being the creakily ancient U.S.T.A.'s designation for the Midwest; farther west were the Southwest, Northwest, and Pacific Northwest sections). My flirtation with tennis excellence had way more to do with the township where I learned and trained and with a weird proclivity for intuitive math than it did with athletic talent. I was, even by the standards of junior competition in which everyone's a bud of pure potential, a pretty untalented tennis player. My hand-eye was OK, but I was neither large nor quick, had a near-concave chest and wrists so thin I could bracelet them with a thumb and pinkie, and could hit a tennis ball no harder or truer than most girls in my age bracket. What I could do was "Play the Whole Court." This was a piece of tennis truistics that could mean any number of things. In my case, it meant I knew my limitations and the limitations of what I stood inside, and adjusted thusly. I was at my very best in bad conditions.

Now, conditions in Central Illinois are from a mathematical perspective interesting and from a tennis perspective bad. The summer heat and wet-mitten humidity, the grotesquely fertile soil that sends grasses and broadleaves up through the courts' surface by main force, the midges that feed on sweat and the mosquitoes that spawn in the fields' furrows and in the conferva-choked ditches that box each field, night tennis next to impossible because the moths and crap-gnats drawn by the sodium lights form a little planet around each tall lamp and the whole lit court surface is aflutter with spastic little shadows.

But mostly wind. The biggest single factor in Central Illinois' quality of outdoor life is wind. There are more local jokes than I can summon about bent weather vanes and leaning barns, more downstate sobriquets for kinds of wind than there are in Malamut for snow. The wind had a personality, a (poor) temper, and, apparently, agendas. The wind blew autumn leaves into intercalated lines and arcs of force so regular you could photograph them for a textbook on Cramer's Rule and the cross-products of curves in 3-space. It molded winter snow into blinding truncheons that buried stalled cars and required citizens to shovel out not only driveways but the sides of homes; a Central Illinois "blizzard" starts only when the snowfall stops and the wind begins. Most people in Philo didn't comb their hair because why bother. Ladies wore those plastic flags tied down over their parlor-jobs so regularly I thought they were required for a real classy coiffure; girls on the East Coast outside with their hair hanging and tossing around looked wanton and nude to me. Wind wind etc. etc.

The people I know from outside it distill the Midwest into blank flatness, black land and fields of green fronds or five-o'clock stubble, gentle swells and declivities that make the topology a sadistic exercise in plotting quadrics, highway vistas so same and dead they drive motorists mad. Those from IN/WI/Northern IL think of their own Midwest as agronomics and commodity futures and corn-detasseling and bean-walking and seed-company caps, apple-cheeked Nordic types, cider and slaughter and football games with white fogbanks of breath exiting helmets. But in the odd central pocket that is Champaign-Urbana, Rantoul, Philo, Mahomet-Seymour, Mattoon, Farmer City, and Tolono, Midwestern life is informed and deformed by wind. Weather-wise, our township is on the eastern upcurrent of what I once heard an atmospherist in brown tweed call a Thermal Anomaly. Something about southward rotations of crisp air off the Great Lakes and muggy southern stuff from Arkansas and Kentucky miscegenating, plus an odd dose of weird zephyrs from the Mississippi valley three hours west. Chicago calls itself the Windy City, but Chicago, one big windbreak, does not know from a true religious-type wind. And meteorologists have nothing to tell people in Philo, who know perfectly well that the real story is that to the west, between us and the Rockies, there is basically nothing tall, and that weird zephyrs and stirs joined breezes and gusts and thermals and downdrafts and whatever out over Nebraska and Kansas and moved east like streams into rivers and jets and military fronts that gathered like avalanches and roared in reverse down pioneer oxtrails, toward our own personal unsheltered asses. The worst was spring, boys' high school tennis season, when the nets would stand out stiff as proud flags and an errant ball would blow clear to the easternmost fence, interrupting play on the next several courts. During a bad blow some of us would get rope out and tell Rob Lord, who was our fifth man in singles and spectrally thin, that we were going to have to tie him down to keep him from becoming a projectile. Autumn, usually about half as bad as spring, was a low constant roar and the massive clicking sound of continents of dry leaves being arranged into force-curves—I'd heard no sound remotely like this megaclicking until I heard, at nineteen, on New Brunswick's Fundy Bay, my first high-tide wave break and get sucked back out over a shore of polished pebbles. Summers were manic and gusty, then often around August deadly calm. The wind would just die some August days, and it was no relief at all; the cessation drove us nuts. Each August, we realized afresh how much the sound of wind had become part of the soundtrack to life in Philo. The sound of wind had become, for me, silence. When it went away, I was left with the squeak of the blood in my head and the aural glitter of all those little eardrum hairs quivering like a drunk in withdrawal. It was months after I moved to western MA before I could really sleep in the pussified whisper of New England's wind-sound.

To your average outsider, Central Illinois looks ideal for sports. The ground, seen from the air, strongly suggests a board game: anally precise squares of dun or khaki cropland all cut and divided by plumb-straight tar roads (in all farmland, roads still seem more like impediments than avenues). In winter, the terrain always looks like Mannington bathroom tile, white quadrangles where bare (snow), black where trees and scrub have shaken free in the wind. From planes, it always looks to me like Monopoly or Life, or a lab maze for rats; then, from ground level, the arrayed fields of feed corn or soybeans, fields furrowed into lines as straight as only an Allis-

Chalmers and sextant can cut them, look laned like sprint tracks or Olympic pools, hashmarked for serious ball, replete with the angles and alleys of serious tennis. My part of the Midwest always looks laid down special, as if planned.

The terrain's strengths are also its weaknesses. Because the land seems so even, designers of clubs and parks rarely bother to roll it flat before laying the asphalt for tennis courts. The result is usually a slight list that only a player who spends a lot of time on the courts will notice. Because tennis courts are for sun- and eye-reasons always laid lengthwise north–south, and because the land in Central Illinois rises very gently as one moves east toward Indiana and the subtle geologic summit that sends rivers doubled back against their own feeders somewhere in the east of that state, the court's forehand half, for a rightie facing north, always seems physically uphill from the backhand—at a tournament in Richmond IN, just over the Ohio line, I noticed the tilt was reversed. The same soil that's so full of humus farmers have to be bought off to keep markets unflooded keeps clay courts chocked with jimson and thistle and volunteer corn, and it splits asphalt courts open with the upward pressure of broadleaf weeds whose pioneer-stock seeds are unthwarted by a half-inch cover of sealant and stone. So that all but the very best maintained courts in the most affluent Illinois districts are their own little rural landscapes, with tufts and cracks and underground-seepage puddles being part of the lay that one plays. A court's cracks always seem to start off to the side of the service box and meander in and back toward the service line. Foliated in pockets, the black cracks, especially against the forest green that contrasts with the barn red of the space outside the lines to signify fair territory, give the courts the eerie look of well-rivered sections of Illinois, seen from back aloft.

A tennis court, 78' × 27', looks, from above, with its slender rectangles of doubles alleys flanking its whole length, like a cardboard carton with flaps folded back. The net, 3.5 feet high at the posts, divides the court widthwise in half; the service lines divide each half again into backcourt and fore-. In the two forecourts, lines that run from the base of the net's center to the service lines divide them into 21' × 13.5' service boxes. The sharply precise divisions and boundaries, together with the fact that—wind and your more exotic-type spins aside—balls can be made to travel in straight lines only, make textbook tennis plane geometry. It is billiards with balls that won't hold still. It is chess on the run. It is to artillery and airstrikes what football is to infantry and attrition.

Tennis-wise, I had two preternatural gifts to compensate for not much physical talent. Make that three. The first was that I always sweated so much that I stayed fairly ventilated in all weathers. Oversweating seems an ambivalent blessing, and it didn't exactly do wonders for my social life in high school, but it meant I could play for hours on a Turkish-bath July day and not flag a bit so long as I drank water and ate salty stuff between matches. I always looked like a drowned man by about game four, but I didn't cramp, vomit, or pass out, unlike the gleaming Peoria kids whose hair never even lost its part right up until their eyes rolled up in their heads and they pitched forward onto the shimmering concrete. A bigger asset still was that I was extremely comfortable inside straight lines. None of the odd geometric claustrophobia that turns some gifted juniors into skittish zoo animals after a while. I found I felt best physically enwebbed in sharp angles, acute bisections, shaved corners. This was environmental. Philo, Illinois, is a cockeyed grid: nine north–south streets against six northeast–southwest, fifty-one gorgeous slanted-cruciform corners (the east and west intersection-angles' tangents could be evaluated integrally in terms of their secants!) around a three-intersection central town common with a tank whose nozzle pointed northwest at Urbana, plus a frozen native son, felled on the Salerno beachhead, whose bronze hand pointed true north. In the late morning, the Salerno guy's statue had a squat black shadow-arm against grass dense enough to putt on; in the evening the sun galvanized his left profile and cast his arm's accusing shadow out to the right, bent at the angle of a stick in a pond. At college it suddenly occurred to me during a quiz that the differential between the direction the statue's hand pointed and the arc of its shadow's rotation was first-order. Anyway, most of my memories of childhood—whether of furrowed acreage, or of a harvester's sentry duty along RR104W, or of the play of sharp shadows against the Legion Hall softball field's dusk—I could now reconstruct on demand with an edge and protractor.

I liked the sharp intercourse of straight lines more than the other kids I grew up with. I think this is because they were natives, whereas I was an infantile transplant from Ithaca, where my dad had Ph.D.'d. So I'd known, even horizontally and semiconsciously as a baby, something different, the tall hills and serpentine one-ways of upstate NY. I'm pretty sure I kept the amorphous mush of curves and swells as a contrasting backlight somewhere down in the lizardy part of my brain, because the Philo children I fought and played with, kids who knew and had known nothing else, saw nothing stark or new-worldish in the township's planar layout, prized nothing crisp. (Except why do I think it significant that so many of them wound up in the military, performing smart right-faces in razor-creased dress blues?)

Unless you're one of those rare mutant virtuosos of raw force, you'll find that competitive tennis, like money pool, requires geometric thinking, the ability to calculate not merely your own angles but the angles of response to your angles. Because the expansion of response-possibilities is quadratic, you are required to think n shots ahead, where n is a hyperbolic function limited by the sinh of opponent's talent and the cosh of the number of shots in the rally so far (roughly). I was good at this. What made me for a while near-great was that I could also admit the differential complication of wind into my calculations; I could think and play octacally. For the wind put curves in the lines and transformed the game into 3-space. Wind did massive damage to many Central Illinois junior players, particularly in the period from April to July when it needed lithium badly, tending to gust without pattern, swirl and backtrack and die and rise, sometimes blowing in one direction at court level

and in another altogether ten feet overhead. The precision in thinking required one to induct trends in percentage, thrust, and retal-
iatory angle—precision our guy and the other townships' volunteer coaches were good at abstracting about with chalk and board,
attaching a pupil's leg to the fence with clothesline to restrict his
arc of movement in practice, placing laundry baskets in different
corners and making us sink ball after ball, taking masking tape and
laying down Chinese boxes within the court's own boxes for drills
and wind sprints—all this theoretical prep went out the window
when sneakers hit actual court in a tournament. The best-planned,
best-hit ball often just blew out of bounds, was the basic unlyrical
problem. It drove some kids near-mad with the caprice and unfair-
ness of it all, and on real windy days these kids, usually with talent
out the bazoo, would have their first apoplectic racket-throwing
tantrum in about the match's third game and lapse into a kind of
sullen coma by the end of the first set, now bitterly *expecting* to
get screwed over by wind, net, tape, sun. I, who was affectionately
known as Slug because I was such a lazy turd in practice, located
my biggest tennis asset in a weird robotic detachment from whatever unfairnesses of wind and weather I couldn't plan for. I couldn't
begin to tell you how many tournament matches I won between the
ages of twelve and fifteen against bigger, faster, more coordinated,
and better-coached opponents simply by hitting balls unimagina-
tively back down the middle of the court in schizophrenic gales,
letting the other kid play with more verve and panache, waiting
for enough of his ambitious balls aimed near the lines to curve or
slide via wind outside the green court and white stripe into the raw
red territory that won me yet another ugly point. It wasn't pretty
or fun to watch, and even with the Illinois wind I never could have
won whole matches this way had the opponent not eventually had
his small nervous breakdown, buckling under the obvious injustice
of losing to a shallow-chested "pusher" because of the shitty rural
courts and rotten wind that rewarded cautious automatism instead
of verve and panache. I was an unpopular player, with good reason. But to say that I did not use verve or imagination was untrue.

Acceptance is its own verve, and it takes imagination for a player to like wind, and I liked wind; or rather I at least felt the wind had some basic right to be there, and found it sort of interesting, and was willing to expand my logistical territory to countenace the devastating effect a 15- to 30-mph stutter-breeze swirling southwest to east would have on my best calculations as to how ambitiously to respond to Joe Perfecthair's topspin drive into my backhand corner.

The Illinois combination of pocked courts, sickening damp, and wind required and rewarded an almost Zen-like acceptance of things as they actually were, on-court. I won a lot. At twelve, I began getting entry to tournaments beyond Philo and Champaign and Danville. I was driven by my parents or by the folks of Gil Antitoi, son of a Canadian-history professor from Urbana, to events like the Central Illinois Open in Decatur, a town built and owned by the A. E. Staley processing concern and so awash in the stink of roasting corn that kids would play with bandannas tied over their mouths and noses; like the Western Closed Qualifier on the ISU campus in Normal; like the McDonald's Junior Open in the serious corn town of Galesburg, way out west by the River; like the Prairie State Open in Pekin, insurance hub and home of Caterpillar Tractor; like the Midwest Junior Clay Courts at a chichi private club in Peoria's pale version of Scarsdale.

Over the next four summers I got to see way more of the state than is normal or healthy, albeit most of this seeing was a blur of travel and crops, looking between nod-outs at sunrises abrupt and terribly candent over the crease between fields and sky (plus you could see any town you were aimed at the very moment it came around the earth's curve, and the only part of Proust that really moved me in college was the early description of the kid's geometric relation to the distant church spire at Combray), riding in station wagons' backseats through Saturday dawns and Sunday sunsets. I got steadily better; Antitoi, unfairly assisted by an early puberty, got radically better.

By the time we were fourteen, Gil Antitoi and I were the Central

Illinois cream of our age bracket, usually seeded one and two at
area tournaments, able to beat all but a couple of even the kids from
the Chicago suburbs who, together with a contingent from Grosse
Pointe MI, usually dominated the Western regional rankings. That
summer the best fourteen-year-old in the nation was a Chicago
kid, Bruce Brescia (whose penchant for floppy white tennis hats,
low socks with bunnytails at the heel, and lurid pastel sweater vests
testified to proclivities that wouldn't dawn on me for several more
years), but Brescia and his henchman, Mark Mees of Zanesville
OH, never bothered to play anything but the Midwestern Clays
and some indoor events in Cook County, being too busy jetting off
to like the Pacific Hardcourts in Ventura and Junior Wimbledon
and all that. I played Brescia just once, in the quarters of an indoor
thing at the Rosemont Horizon in 1977, and the results were not
pretty. Antitoi actually got a set off Mees in the national Qualifiers
one year. Neither Brescia nor Mees ever turned pro; I don't know
what happened to either of them after eighteen.

Antitoi and I ranged over the exact same competitive territory;
he was my friend and foe and bane. Though I'd started playing two
years before he, he was bigger, quicker, and basically better than I
by about age thirteen, and I was soon losing to him in the finals of
just about every tournament I played. So different were our appear-
ances and approaches and general gestalts that we had something
of an epic rivalry from '74 through '77. I had gotten so prescient at
using stats, surface, sun, gusts, and a kind of stoic cheer that I was
regarded as a kind of physical savant, a medicine boy of wind and
heat, and could play just forever, sending back moonballs baroque
with spin. Antitoi, uncomplicated from the get-go, hit the everliving shit out of every round object that came within his ambit,
aiming always for one of two backcourt corners. He was a Slugger;
I was a Slug. When he was "on," i.e. having a good day, he varnished
the court with me. When he wasn't at his best (and the countless
hours I and David Saboe from Bloomington and Kirk Riehagen and
Steve Cassil of Danville spent in meditation and seminar on just
what variables of diet, sleep, romance, car ride, and even sock-color

factored into the equation of Antitoi's mood and level day to day), he and I had great matches, real marathon wind-suckers. Of eleven finals we played in 1974, I won two.

Midwest junior tennis was also my initiation into true adult sadness. I had developed a sort of hubris about my Taoistic ability to control via noncontrol. I'd established a private religion of wind. I even liked to bike. Awfully few people in Philo bike, for obvious wind reasons, but I'd found a way to sort of tack back and forth against a stiff current, holding some wide book out at my side at about 120° to my angle of thrust—Baynes and Pugh's *The Art of the Engineer* and Cheiro's *Language of the Hand* proved to be the best airfoils—so that through imagination and verve and stoic cheer I could not just neutralize but use an in-your-face gale for biking. Similarly, by thirteen I'd found a way not just to accommodate but to *employ* the heavy summer winds in matches. No longer just mooning the ball down the center to allow plenty of margin for error and swerve, I was now able to use the currents kind of the way a pitcher uses spit. I could hit curves way out into cross-breezes that'd drop the ball just fair; I had a special wind-serve that had so much spin the ball turned oval in the air and curved left to right like a smart slider and then reversed its arc on the bounce. I'd developed the same sort of autonomic feel for what the wind would do to the ball that a standard-trans driver has for how to shift. As a junior tennis player, I was for a time a citizen of the concrete physical world in a way the other boys weren't, I felt. And I felt betrayed at around fourteen when so many of these single-minded flailing boys became abruptly mannish and tall, with sudden sprays of hair on their thighs and wisps on their lips and ropy arteries on their forearms. My fifteenth summer, kids I'd been beating easily the year before all of a sudden seemed overpowering. I lost in two semifinals, at Pekin and Springfield in '77, of events I'd beaten Antitoi in the finals of in '76. My dad just about brought me to my knees after the Springfield loss to some kid from the Quad Cities when he said, trying to console me, that it had looked like a boy playing a man out there. And the other boys sensed something up with me, too, smelled some breakdown in the odd détente I'd had with the elements: my ability to accommodate and fashion the exterior was being undercut by the malfunction of some internal alarm clock I didn't understand.

I mention this mostly because so much of my Midwest's communal psychic energy was informed by growth and fertility. The agronomic angle was obvious, what with my whole township dependent for tax base on seed, dispersion, height, and yield. Something about the adults' obsessive weighing and measuring and projecting, this special calculus of thrust and growth, leaked inside us children's capped and bandanna'd little heads out on the fields, diamonds, and courts of our special interests. By 1977 I was the only one of my group of jock friends with virginity intact. (I know this for a fact, and only because these guys are now schoolteachers and commoditists and insurers with families and standings to protect will I not share with you just how I know it.) I felt, as I became a later and later bloomer, alienated not just from my own recalcitrant glabrous little body, but in a way from the whole elemental exterior I'd come to see as my coconspirator. I knew, somehow, that the call to height and hair came from outside, from whatever apart from Monsanto and Dow made the corn grow, the hogs rut, the wind soften every spring and hang with the scent of manure from the plain of beanfields north between us and Champaign. My vocation ebbed. I felt uncalled. I began to experience the same resentment toward whatever children abstract as nature that I knew Steve Cassil felt when a soundly considered approach shot down the forehand line was blown out by a gust, that I knew Gil Antitoi suffered when his pretty kick-serve (he was the only top-flight kid from the slow weedy township courts to play serve-and-volley from the start, which is why he had such success on the slick cement of the West Coast when he went on to play for Cal Fullerton) was compromised by the sun: he was so tall, and so stubborn about adjusting his high textbook service toss for solar conditions, that serving from the court's north end in early afternoon matches always filled his eyes with violet blobs, and he'd lumber around for the rest of the point, flailing and pissed. This was back when sunglasses were unheard of, on-court.

But so the point is I began to feel what they'd felt. I began, very quietly, to resent my physical place in the great schema, and this resentment and bitterness, a kind of slow root-rot, is a big reason why I never qualified for the sectional championships again after 1977, and why I ended up in 1980 barely making the team at a college smaller than Urbana High while kids I had beaten and then envied played scholarship tennis for Purdue, Fullerton, Michigan, Pepperdine, and even—in the case of Pete Bouton, who grew half a foot and forty IQ points in 1977—for the hallowed U of I at Urbana-Champaign.

Alienation-from-Midwest-as-fertility-grid might be a little on the overmetaphysical side, not to mention self-pitying. This was the time, after all, when I discovered definite integrals and antiderivatives and found my identity shifting from jock to math-wienie anyway. But it's also true that my whole Midwest tennis career matured and then degenerated under the aegis of the Peter Principle. In and around my township—where the courts were rural and budgets low and conditions so extreme that the mosquitoes sounded like trumpets and the bees like tubas and the wind like a five-alarm fire, that we had to change shirts between games and use our water jugs to wash blown field-chaff off our arms and necks and carry salt tablets in Pez containers—I was truly near-great: I could Play the Whole Court; I was In My Element. But all the more important tournaments, the events into which my rural excellence was an easement, were played in a different real world: the courts' surface was redone every spring at the Arlington Tennis Center, where the National Junior Qualifier for our region was held; the green of these courts' fair territory was so vivid as to distract, its surface so new and rough it wrecked your feet right through your shoes, and so bare of flaw, tilt, crack, or seam that it was totally disorienting. Playing on a perfect court was for me like treading water out of sight of land: I never knew where I was out there. The 1976 Chicago Junior Invitational was held at Lincolnshire's Bath and

Tennis Club, whose huge warren of thirty-six courts was enclosed by all these troubling green plastic tarps attached to all the fences, with little archer-slits in them at eye level to afford some parody of spectation. These tarps were Wind-B-Gone windscreens, patented by the folks over at Cyclone Fence in 1971. They did cut down on the worst of the unfair gusts, but they also seemed to rob the court space of new air: competing at Lincolnshire was like playing in the bottom of a well. And blue bug-zapper lights festooned the lightposts when really major Midwest tournaments played into the night: no clouds of midges around the head or jagged shadows of moths to distinguish from balls' flights, but a real unpleasant zotting and frying sound of bugs being decommissioned just overhead; I won't pause to mention the smell. The point is I just wasn't the same, somehow, without deformities to play around. I'm thinking now that the wind and bugs and chuckholes formed for me a kind of inner boundary, my own personal set of lines. Once I hit a certain level of tournament facilities, I was disabled because I was unable to accommodate the absence of disabilities to accommodate. If that makes sense. Puberty-angst and material alienation notwithstanding, my Midwest tennis career plateaued the moment I saw my first windscreen.

Still strangely eager to speak of weather, let me say that my township, in fact all of East-Central Illinois, is a proud part of what meteorologists call Tornado Alley. Incidence of tornadoes all out of statistical proportion. I personally have seen two on the ground and five aloft, trying to assemble. Aloft tornadoes are gray-white, more like convulsions in the thunderclouds themselves than separate or protruding from them. Ground tornadoes are black only because of the tons of soil they suck in and spin around. The grotesque frequency of tornadoes around my township is, I'm told, a function of the same variables that cause our civilian winds: we are a coordinate where fronts and air masses converge. Most days from late March to June there are Tornado Watches somewhere in our TV stations' viewing area (the stations put a little graphic at the screen's upper right, like a pair of binoculars for a Watch and the Tarot deck's Tower card for a Warning, or something). Watches mean conditions are right and so on and so forth, which, big deal. It's only the rarer Tornado Warnings, which require a confirmed sighting by somebody with reliable sobriety, that make the Civil Defense sirens go. The siren on top of the Philo Middle School was a different pitch and cycle from the one off in the south part of Urbana, and the two used to weave in and out of each other in a godawful threnody. When the sirens blew, the native families went to their canning cellars or fallout shelters (no kidding); the academic families in their bright prefab houses with new lawns and foundations of flat slab went with whatever good-luck tokens they could lay hands on to the very most central point on the ground floor after opening every single window to thwart implosion from precipitous pressure drops. For my family, the very most central point was a hallway between my dad's study and a linen closet, with a reproduction of a Flemish annunciation scene on one wall and a bronze Aztec sunburst hanging with guillotinic mass on the other; I always tried to maneuver my sister under the sunburst.

If there was an actual Warning when you were outside and away from home—say at a tennis tournament in some godforsaken public park at some city fringe zoned for sprawl—you were supposed to lie prone in the deepest depression you could locate. Since the only real depressions around most tournament sites were the irrigation and runoff ditches that bordered cultivated fields, ditches icky with conferva and mosquito spray and always heaving with what looked like conventions of copperheads and just basically places your thinking man doesn't lie prone in under any circumstance, in practice at Warned tournament you zipped your rackets into their covers and ran to find your loved ones or even your liked ones and just all milled around trying to look like you weren't about to lose sphincter-control. Mothers tended sometimes to wail and clutch childish heads to their bosoms (Mrs. Swearingen of Pekin was particularly popular for clutching even strange kids' heads to her formidable bosom).

I mention tornadoes for reasons directly related to the purpose of this essay. For one thing, they were a real part of Midwest childhood, because as a little kid I was obsessed with dread over them. My earliest nightmares, the ones that didn't feature mile-high robots from *Lost in Space* wielding huge croquet mallets (don't ask), were about shrieking sirens and dead white skies, a slender monster on the Iowa horizon, jutting less phallic than saurian from the lowering sky, whipping back and forth with such frenzy that it almost doubled on itself, trying to eat its own tail. Throwing off chaff and dust and chairs; it never came any closer than the horizon; it didn't have to.

In practice, Watches and Warnings both seemed to have a kind of boy-and-wolf quality for the natives of Philo. They just happened too often. Watches seemed especially irrelevant, because we could always see storms coming from the west way in advance, and by the time they were over, say, Decatur you could diagnose the basic condition by the color and height of the clouds: the taller the anvil-shaped thunderheads, the better the chance for hail and Warnings; pitch-black clouds were a happier sight than gray shot with an odd nacreous white; the shorter the interval between the sight of lightning and the sound of thunder, the faster the system was moving, and the faster the system, the worse: like most things that mean you harm, severe thunderstorms are brisk and no-nonsense.

I know why I stayed obsessed as I aged. Tornadoes, for me, were a transfiguration. Like all serious winds, they were our little stretch of plain's z coordinate, a move up from the Euclidian monotone of furrow, road, axis, and grid. We studied tornadoes in junior high: a Canadian high straight-lines it southeast from the Dakotas; a moist warm mass drawls on up north from like Arkansas: the result was not a Greek χ or even a Cartesian Γ but a circling of the square, a curling of vectors, concavation of curves. It was alchemical, Leibnizian. Tornadoes were, in our part of Central Illinois, the dimensionless point at which parallel lines met and whirled and blew up. They made no sense. Houses blew not out but in. Brothels were spared while orphanages next door bought it. Dead cattle were found three miles from their silage without a scratch on them. Tornadoes are omnipotent and obey no law. Force without law has no shape, only tendency and duration. I believe now that I knew all this without knowing it, as a kid.

The only time I ever got caught in what might have been an actual one was in June '78 on a tennis court at Hessel Park in Champaign, where I was drilling one afternoon with Gil Antitoi. Though a contemptible and despised tournament opponent, I was a coveted practice partner because I could transfer balls to wherever you wanted them with the mindless constancy of a machine. This particular day it was supposed to rain around suppertime, and a couple times we thought we'd heard the tattered edges of a couple sirens out west toward Monticello, but Antitoi and I drilled religiously every afternoon that week on the slow clayish Har-Tru of Hessel, trying to prepare for a beastly clay invitational in Chicago where it was rumored both Brescia and Mees would appear. We were doing butterfly drills—my crosscourt forehand is transferred back down the line to Antitoi's backhand, he crosscourts it to my backhand, I send it down the line to his forehand, four 45° angles, though the intersection of just his crosscourts make an X, which is four 90's and also a crucifix rotated the same quarter-turn that a swastika (which involves eight 90° angles) is rotated on Hitlerian bunting. This was the sort of stuff that went through my head when I drilled. Hessel Park was scented heavily with cheese from the massive Kraft factory at Champaign's western limit, and it had wonderful expensive soft Har-Tru courts of such a deep piney color that the flights of the fluorescent balls stayed on one's visual screen for a few extra seconds, leaving trails, is also why the angles and hieroglyphs involved in butterfly drill seem important. But the crux here is that butterflies are primarily a conditioning drill: both players have to get from one side of the court to the other between each stroke, and once the initial pain and wind-sucking are over—assuming you're a kid who's in absurd shape because he spends countless mindless hours jumping rope or running laps backward or doing star-drills between the court's corners or straight sprints back and forth along the perfect furrows of early beanfields each morning—once the first pain and fatigue of butterflies are got through, if both guys are good enough so that there are few unforced errors to break up the rally, a kind of fugue-state opens up inside you where your concentration telescopes toward a still point and you lose awareness of your limbs and the soft shush of your shoe's slide (you have to slide out of a run on Har-Tru) and whatever's outside the lines of the court, and pretty much all you know then is the bright ball and the octangled butterfly outline of its trail across the billiard green of the court. We had one just endless rally and I'd left the planet in a silent swoop inside when the court and ball and butterfly trail all seemed to surge brightly and glow as the daylight just plain went out in the sky overhead. Neither of us had noticed that there'd been no wind blowing the familiar grit into our eyes for several minutes—a bad sign. There was no siren. Later they said the C.D. alert network had been out of order. This was June 6, 1978. The air temperature dropped so fast you could feel your hairs rise. There was no thunder and no air stirred. I could not tell you why we kept hitting. Neither of us said anything. There was no siren. It was high noon; there was nobody else on the courts. The riding mower out over east at the softball field was still going back and forth. There were no depressions except a saprogenic ditch along the field of new corn just west. What could we have done? The air always smells of mowed grass before a bad storm. I think we thought it would rain at worst and that we'd play till it rained and then go sit in Antitoi's parents' station wagon. I do remember a mental obscenity—I had gut strings in my rackets, strings everybody with a high sectional ranking got free for letting the Wilson sales rep spray-paint a *W* across the racket face, so they were free, but I liked this particular string job on this racket, I liked them tight but not real tight, 62–63 p.s.i. on a Pro-Flite stringer, and gut becomes pasta if it gets wet, but we were both in the fugue-state that exhaustion through repetition brings on, a fugue-state I've decided that my whole time playing tennis was spent chasing, a fugue-state I associated too with plowing and seeding and detasseling and spreading herbicides back and forth in sentry duty along perfect lines, up and back, or military marching on flat blacktop, hypnotic, a mental state at once flat and lush, numbing and yet exquisitely felt. We were young, we didn't know when to stop. Maybe I was mad at my body and wanted to hurt it, wear it down. Then the whole knee-high field to the west along Kirby Avenue all of a sudden flattened out in a wave coming toward us as if the field was getting steamrolled. Antitoi went wide west for a forehand cross and I saw the corn get laid down in waves and the sycamores in a copse lining the ditch point our way. There was no funnel. Either it had just materialized and come down or it wasn't a real one. The big heavy swings on the industrial swingsets took off, wrapping themselves in their chains around and around the top crossbar; the park's grass laid down the same way the field had; the whole thing happened so fast I'd seen nothing like it; recall that Bimini H-Bomb film of the shock wave visible in the sea as it comes toward the ship's film crew. This all happened very fast but in serial progression: field, trees, swings, grass, then the feel like the lift of the world's biggest mitt, the nets suddenly and sexually up and out straight, and I seem to remember whacking a ball out of my hand at Antitoi to watch its radical west–east curve, and for some reason trying to run after this ball I'd just hit, but I couldn't have tried to run after a ball I had hit, but I remember the heavy gentle lift at my thighs and the ball curving back closer and my passing the ball and beating the ball in flight over the horizontal net, my feet not once touching the ground over fifty-odd feet, a cartoon, and then there was chaff and crud in the air all over and both Antitoi and I either flew or were blown pinwheeling for I swear it must have been fifty feet to the fence one court over, the easternmost fence, we hit the fence so hard we knocked it halfway down, and it stuck at 45°, Antitoi detached a retina and had to wear those funky Jabbar retina-goggles for the rest of the summer, and the fence had two body-shaped indentations like in cartoons where the guy's face makes a cast in the skillet that hit him, two catcher's masks of fence, we both got deep quadrangular lines impressed on our faces, torsos, legs' fronts, from the fence, my sister said we looked like waffles, but neither of us got badly hurt, and no homes got whacked—either the thing just ascended again for no reason right after, they do that, obey no rule, follow no line, hop up and down at something that might as well be will, or else it wasn't a real one. Antitoi's tennis continued to improve after that, but mine didn't.

1991

How Tracy Austin
Broke My Heart

B ECAUSE I AM a long-time rabid fan of tennis in general
and Tracy Austin in particular, I've rarely looked forward to
reading a sports memoir the way I looked forward to Ms. Austin's
Beyond Center Court: My Story, ghosted by Christine Brennan and
published by Morrow. This is a type of mass-market book—the
sports-star-"with"-somebody autobiography—that I seem to have
bought and read an awful lot of, with all sorts of ups and downs
and ambivalence and embarrassment, usually putting these books
under something more highbrow when I get to the register. I think
Austin's memoir has maybe finally broken my jones for the genre,
though.

Here's *Beyond Center Court*'s Austin on the first set of her final
against Chris Evert at the 1979 U.S. Open: "At 2–3, I broke Chris,
then she broke me, and I broke her again, so we were at 4–4."

And on her epiphany after winning that final: "I immediately
knew what I had done, which was win the U.S. Open, and I was
thrilled."

Tracy Austin on the psychic rigors of pro competition: "Every
professional athlete has to be so fine-tuned mentally."

Tracy Austin on her parents: "My mother and father never, ever
pushed me."

Tracy Austin on Martina Navratilova: "She is a wonderful person, very sensitive and caring."

On Billie Jean King: "She also is incredibly charming and
accommodating."

On Brooke Shields: "She was so sweet and bright and easy to talk to right away."

Tracy Austin meditating on excellence: "There is that little bit extra that some of us are willing to give and some of us aren't. Why is that? I think it's the challenge to be the best."

You get the idea. On the upside, though, this breathtakingly insipid autobiography can maybe help us understand both the seduction and the disappointment that seem to be built into the mass-market sports memoir. Almost uniformly poor as books, these athletic "My Story"s sell incredibly well; that's why there are so many of them. And they sell so well because athletes' stories seem to promise something more than the regular old name-dropping celebrity autobiography.

Here is a theory. Top athletes are compelling because they embody the comparison-based achievement we Americans revere—fast*est*, strong*est*—and because they do so in a totally unambiguous way. Questions of the best plumber or best managerial accountant are impossible even to define, whereas the best relief pitcher, free-throw shooter, or female tennis player is, at any given time, a matter of public statistical record. Top athletes fascinate us by appealing to our twin compulsions with competitive superiority and hard data.

Plus they're beautiful: Jordan hanging in midair like a Chagall bride, Sampras laying down a touch volley at an angle that defies Euclid. And they're inspiring. There is about world-class athletes carving out exemptions from physical laws a transcendent beauty that makes manifest God in man. So actually more than one theory, then. Great athletes are profundity in motion. They enable abstractions like *power* and *grace* and *control* to become not only incarnate but televisable. To be a top athlete, performing, is to be that exquisite hybrid of animal and angel that we average unbeautiful watchers have such a hard time seeing in ourselves.

So we want to know them, these gifted, driven physical achievers. We too, as audience, are driven: watching the performance is not enough. We want to get intimate with all that profundity.

We want inside them; we want the Story. We want to hear about humble roots, privation, precocity, grim resolve, discouragement, persistence, team spirit, sacrifice, killer instinct, liniment and pain. We want to know how they did it. How many hours a night did the child Bird spend in his driveway hitting jumpers under home-strung floodlights? What ungodly time did Björn get up for practice every morning? What exact makes of cars did the Butkus boys work out by pushing up and down Chicago streets? What did Palmer and Brett and Payton and Evert have to give up? And of course, too, we want to know how it *feels*, inside, to be both beautiful and best ("How did it feel to win the big one?"). What combination of blank-ness and concentration is required to sink a putt or a free throw for thousands of dollars in front of millions of unblinking eyes? What goes through their minds? Are these athletes real people? Are they even remotely like us? Is their Agony of Defeat anything like our little agonies of daily frustration? And of course what about the Thrill of Victory—what might it feel like to hold up that #1 finger and be able to actually *mean* it?

I am about the same age and played competitive tennis in the same junior ranks as Tracy Austin, half a country away and several plateaus below her. When we all heard, in 1977, that a California girl who'd just turned fourteen had won a professional tourna-ment in Portland, we weren't so much jealous as agog. None of us could come close to testing even a top eighteen-year-old, much less pro-caliber adults. We started to hunt her up in tennis maga-zines, search out her matches on obscure cable channels. She was about 4'6" and 85 pounds. She hit the hell out of the ball and never missed and never choked and had braces and pigtails that swung wildly around as she handed pros their asses. She was the first real child star in women's tennis, and in the late '70s she was prodigious, beautiful, and inspiring. There was an incongruously adult genius about her game, all the more radiant for her little-girl giggle and silly hair. I remember meditating, with all the intensity a fifteen-year-old can summon, on the differences that kept this girl and me on our respective sides of the TV screen. She was a genius and I was not. How must it have felt? I had some serious questions to ask her. I wanted, very much, her side of it.

So the point, then, about these sports memoirs' market appeal: Because top athletes are profound, because they make a certain type of genius as carnally discernible as it ever can get, these ghost-written invitations inside their lives and their skulls are terribly seductive for book buyers. Explicitly or not, the memoirs make a promise—to let us penetrate the indefinable mystery of what makes some persons geniuses, semidivine, to share with us the secret and so both to reveal the difference between us and them and to erase it, a little, that difference . . . to give us the (we want, expect, only one, the master narrative, the key) Story.

However seductively they promise, though, these autobiographies rarely deliver. And *Beyond Center Court: My Story* is especially bad. The book fails not so much because it's poorly written (which it is—I don't know what ghostwriter Brennan's enhancing function was supposed to be here, but it's hard to see how Austin herself could have done any worse than two hundred dead pages of "Tennis took me like a magic carpet to all kinds of places and all kinds of people" enlivened only by wincers like "Injuries—the signature of the rest of my career—were about to take hold of me"), but because it commits what any college sophomore knows is the capital crime of expository prose: it forgets who it's supposed to be for.

Obviously, a good commercial memoir's first loyalty has got to be to the reader, the person who's spending money and time to access the consciousness of someone he wishes to know and will never meet. But none of *Beyond Center Court*'s loyalties are to the reader. The author's primary allegiance seems to be to her family and friends. Whole pages are given over to numbing Academy Award–style tributes to parents, siblings, coaches, trainers, and agents, plus little burbles of praise for pretty much every athlete and celebrity she's ever met. In particular, Austin's account of her own (extremely, transcendently interesting) competitive career keeps digressing into warm fuzzies on each opponent she faces.

Typical example: Her third round at 1980's Wimbledon was against American Barbara Potter, who, we learn,

> is a really good person. Barbara was very nice to me through my injuries, sending me books, keeping in touch, and checking to see how I was doing. Barbara definitely was one of the smartest people on the tour; I've heard she's going to college now, which takes a lot of initiative for a woman our age. Knowing Barbara, I'm sure she's working harder than all her fellow students.

But there is also here an odd loyalty to and penchant for the very clichés with which we sports fans weave the veil of myth and mystery that these sports memoirs promise to part for us. It's almost as if Tracy Austin has structured her own sense of her life and career to accord with the formulas of the generic sports bio. We've got the sensitive and doting mother, the kindly dad, the mischievous siblings who treat famous Tracy like just another kid. We've got the ingenue heroine whose innocence is eroded by experience and transcended through sheer grit; we've got the gruff but tenderhearted coach and the coolly skeptical veterans who finally accept the heroine. We've got the wicked, backstabbing rival (in Pam Shriver, who receives the book's only unfulsome mention). We even get the myth-requisite humble roots. Austin, whose father is a corporate scientist and whose mother is one of those lean tan ladies who seem to spend all day every day at the country club tennis courts, tries to portray her childhood in posh Rolling Hills Estates CA as impoverished: "We had to be frugal in all kinds of ways . . . we cut expenses by drinking powdered milk . . . we didn't have bacon except on Christmas." Stuff like this seems way out of touch with reality until we realize that the kind of reality the author's chosen to be in touch with here is not just un- but anti-real.

In fact, as unrevealing of character as its press-release tone and generic-myth structure make this memoir, it's the narrator's cluelessness that permits us our only glimpses of anything like a real and faceted life. That is, relief from the book's skewed loyalties can be found only in those places where the author seems unwittingly to betray them. She protests, for instance, repeatedly and with an almost Gertrudian fervor, that her mother "did not force" her into tennis at age three, it apparently never occurring to Tracy Austin that a three-year-old hasn't got enough awareness of choices to require any forcing. This was the child of a mom who'd spent the evening before Tracy's birth hitting tennis balls to the family's other four children, three of whom also ended up playing pro tennis. Many of the memoir's recollections of Mrs. Austin seem almost Viennese in their repression—"My mother always made sure I behaved on court, but I never even considered acting up"—and downright creepy are some of the details Austin chooses in order to evince "how nonintense my tennis background really was":

> Everyone thinks every young tennis player is very one-dimensional, which just wasn't true in my case. Until I was fourteen, I never played tennis on Monday. . . . My mother made sure I never put in seven straight days on the court. She didn't go to the club on Mondays, so we never went there.

It gets weirder. Later in the book's childhood section, Austin discusses her "wonderful friendship" with a man from their country club who "set up . . . matches for me against unsuspecting foes in later years and . . . won a lot of money from his friends" and, as a token of friendship, "bought me a necklace with a *T* hanging on it. The *T* had fourteen diamonds in it." She was apparently ten at this point. As the book's now fully adult Austin analyzes the relationship, "He was a very wealthy criminal lawyer, and I didn't have very much money. With all his gifts for me, he made me feel special." What a guy. Regarding her de facto employment in what is technically known as sports hustling: "It was all in good fun."

In the subsequent section, Austin recalls a 1978 pro tournament in Japan that she hadn't much wanted to enter:

It was just too far from home and I was tired from the travel grind. They kept offering me more and more money for an appearance fee—well over a hundred thousand dollars—but I said no. Finally, they offered to fly my whole family over. That did it. We went, and I won easily.

Besides displaying an odd financial sense (she won't come for $100,000+, but will come if they add a couple thousand in airfare?), Tracy Austin seems here unaware of the fact that, in the late '70s, any player who accepted a guaranteed payment just for entering a tournament was in violation of a serious tour rule. The backstory here is that both genders' player associations had outlawed these payments because they threatened both the real and the perceived integrity of pro tennis. A tournament that has paid some star player a hefty guarantee—wanting her in the draw because her celebrity will help increase ticket sales, corporate sponsorships, TV revenues, etc.—thereafter has an obvious stake in that player's survival in the tournament, and so has an equally obvious interest in keeping her from getting upset by some lesser-known player in the early rounds, which, since matches' linesmen and umpires are employed by the tournament, can lead to shady officiating. And has so led. Far stranger things than a marquee player's receiving a suspicious number of favorable line calls have happened . . . though apparently somehow not in Tracy Austin's experience.

The naïveté on display throughout this memoir is doubly confusing. On the one hand, there's little sign in this narrator of anything like the frontal-lobe activity required for outright deception. On the other, Austin's ignorance of her sport's grittier realities seems literally incredible. Random examples. When she sees a player "tank" a 1988 tournament match to make time for a lucrative appearance in a TV ad, Tracy "couldn't believe it. . . . I had never played with anyone who threw a match before, so it took me a set and a half to realize what was happening." This even though match-tanking had been widely and publicly reported as a dark consequence of skyrocketing exhibition and endorsement fees for at least the eleven years Austin had been in pro tennis. Or, drugs-wise, although problems with everything up to cocaine and heroin in pro tennis had been not only acknowledged but written about in the 1980s,[1] Austin manages to move the reader to both scorn and pity with pronouncements like "I assume players were experimenting with marijuana, but I don't know who or when or where. I wasn't invited to those parties, if they were happening at all. And I'm very glad I wasn't." And so on and so on.

Ultimately, though, what makes *Beyond Center Court* so especially disappointing is that it could have been much more than just another I-was-born-to-play sports memoir. The facts of Tracy Austin's life and its trajectory are almost classically tragic. She was the first of tennis's now-ubiquitous nymphet prodigies, and her rise was meteoric. Picked out of the crowd as a toddler by coaching guru Vic Braden, Austin was on the cover of *World Tennis* magazine at age four. She played her first junior tournament at seven, and by ten she had won the national girls' twelve-and-under championship both indoors and out- and was being invited to play public exhibitions. At thirteen she had won national titles in most junior age-groups, been drafted as a professional by World Team Tennis, and appeared on the cover of *Sports Illustrated* under the teaser "A Star Is Born." At fourteen, having chewed up every female in U.S. juniors, she entered the preliminary qualifiers for her first professional tournament and proceeded to win not just the qualifying event but the whole tourney—a feat roughly equivalent to someone who was ineligible for a DMV learner's permit winning the Indianapolis 500. She played Wimbledon at fourteen, turned pro as a ninth-grader, won the U.S. Open at sixteen, and was ranked number one in the world at just seventeen, in 1980. This was the same year her body started to fall apart. She spent the next four years effectively crippled by injuries and bizarre accidents, playing

---

1. AP reporter Michael Mewshaw's *Short Circuit* (Atheneum, 1983) is just one example of national-press stuff about drugs on the tour.

sporadically and watching her ranking plummet, and was for all practical purposes retired from tennis at age twenty-one. In 1989, her one serious attempt at a comeback ended on the way to the U.S. Open, when a speeder ran a red light and nearly killed her. She is now, as of this writing, a professional former sports star, running celebrity clinics for corporate sponsors and doing sad little bits of color commentary on some of the same cable channels I'd first seen her play on.

What's nearly Greek about her career's arc is that Tracy Austin's most conspicuous virtue, a relentless workaholic perfectionism that combined with raw talent to make her such a prodigious success, turned out to be also her flaw and bane. She was, even after puberty, a tiny person, and her obsessive practice regimen and uncompromising effort in every last match began to afflict her with what sports M.D.s now know to be simple consequences of hypertrophy and chronic wear: hamstring and hip flexor pulls, sciatica, scoliosis, tendinitis, stress fractures, plantar fasciitis. Then too, since woe classically breeds more woe, she was freak-accident-prone: coaches who fall on her while ice-skating and break her ankle, psychotic chiropractors who pull her spine out of alignment, waiters who splash her with scalding water, color-blind speeders on the JFK Parkway.

A successful Tracy Austin autobiography, then, could have afforded us plain old plumbers and accountants more than just access to the unquestioned genius of an athletic savant or her high-speed ascent to the top of a univocal, mathematically computed hierarchy. This book could actually have helped us to countenance the sports myth's dark side. The only thing Tracy Austin had ever known how to do, her art—what the tragic-savvy Greeks would have called her *technē*, that state in which Austin's mastery of craft facilitated a communion with the gods themselves—was removed from her at an age when most of us are just starting to think seriously about committing ourselves to some pursuit. This memoir could have been about both the seductive immortality of competitive success and the less seductive but way more significant fragility and impermanence of all the competitive venues in which mortal humans chase immortality. Austin's story could, since the predicament of a dedicated athletic prodigy washed up at twenty-one differs in nothing more than degree from that of a dedicated CPA and family man dying at sixty-two, have been profound. The book could, since having it all at seventeen and then losing it all by twenty-one because of stuff outside your control is just like death except you have to go on living afterward, have been truly inspirational. And the publisher's flap copy promises just this: "The inspirational story of Tracy Austin's long struggle to find a life beyond championship tennis."

But the publisher's flap copy lies, because it turns out that *inspirational* is being used on the book jacket only in its ad-cliché sense, one basically equivalent to *heartwarming* or *feel-good* or even (God forbid) *triumphant*. Like all good ad clichés, it manages to suggest everything and mean nothing. Honorably used, *to inspire* means, according to Mr. American Heritage, "to animate the mind or emotions of; to communicate by divine influence." Which is to say that *inspirational*, honorably used, describes precisely what a great athlete becomes when she's in the arena performing, sharing the particular divinity she's given her life for, letting people witness concrete, transient instantiations of a grace that for most of us remains abstract and immanent.

Transcendent as were Tracy Austin's achievements on a public court, her autobiography does not come anywhere close to honoring the promise of its flap copy's "inspirational." Because forget divine—there's not even a recognizable human being in here. And this isn't just because of clunky prose or luxated structure. The book is inanimate because it communicates no real feeling and so gives us no sense of a conscious person. There's nobody at the other end of the line. Every emotionally significant moment or event or development gets conveyed in either computeresque staccato or else a prepackaged PR-speak whose whole function is (think about it) to deaden feeling. See, for instance, Austin's account of the moment when she has just beaten a world-class adult to win her first professional tournament:

> It was a tough match and I simply outlasted her. I was beginning to get a reputation for doing that. When you play from the baseline, perseverance is everything. The prize money for first place was twenty-eight thousand dollars.[2]

Or check out the book's description of her career's tragic climax. After working for five years to make a comeback and then, literally on the way to Flushing Meadows' National Tennis Center, getting sideswiped by a van and having her leg shattered through sheer bad luck, Tracy Austin was now permanently finished as a world-class athlete, and had then to lie for weeks in traction and think about the end of the only life she'd ever known. In *Beyond Center Court*, Austin's inspirational prose-response to this consists of quoting Leo Buscaglia, reporting on her newfound enthusiasm for shopping, and then giving us an excruciating chapter-long list of every celebrity she's ever met.

Of course, neither Austin nor her book is unique. It's hard not to notice the way this same air of robotic banality suffuses not only the sports-memoir genre but also the media rituals in which a top athlete is asked to describe the content or meaning of his *technē*. Turn on any post-contest TV interview: "Kenny, how did it feel to make that sensational game-winning shoestring catch in the end zone with absolutely no I mean *zero* time remaining on the clock?" "Well, Frank, I was just real pleased. I was real happy and also pleased. We've all worked hard and come a long way as a team, and it's always a good feeling to be able to contribute." "Mark, you've now

2. Or listen again to her report of how winning her first U.S. Open felt: "I immediately knew what I had done, which was win the U.S. Open, and I was thrilled." This line haunts me; it's like the whole letdown of the book boiled down into one dead bite.

homered in your last eight straight at-bats and lead both leagues in RBIs—any comment?" "Well, Bob, I'm just trying to take it one pitch at a time. I've been focusing on the fundamentals, you know, and trying to make a contribution, and all of us know we've got to take it one game at a time and hang in there and not look ahead and just basically do the best we can at all times." This stuff is stupefying, and yet it also seems to be inevitable, maybe even necessary. The baritones in network blazers keep coming up after games, demanding of physical geniuses these recombinant strings of dead clichés, strings that after a while start to sound like a strange kind of lullaby, and which of course no network would solicit and broadcast again and again if there weren't a large and serious audience out here who find the banalities right and good. As if the emptiness in these athletes' descriptions of their feelings confirmed something we need to believe.

All right, so the obvious point: Great athletes usually turn out to be stunningly inarticulate about just those qualities and experiences that constitute their fascination. For me, though, the important question is why this is always so bitterly disappointing. And why I keep buying these sports memoirs with expectations that my own experience with the genre should long ago have modified . . . and why I nearly always feel thwarted and pissed when I finish them. One sort of answer, of course, is that commercial autobiographies like these promise something they cannot deliver: personal and verbal access to an intrinsically public and performative kind of genius. The problem with this answer is that I and the rest of the U.S. book market aren't that stupid—if impossible promises were all there was to it, we'd catch on after a while, and it would stop being so profitable for publishers to churn these memoirs out.

Maybe what keeps us buying in the face of constant disappointment is some deep compulsion both to experience genius in the concrete and to universalize genius in the abstract. Real indisputable genius is so impossible to define, and true *technē* so rarely visible (much less televisable), that maybe we automatically expect people who are geniuses as athletes to be geniuses also as speakers and writers, to be articulate, perceptive, truthful, profound. If it's just that we naïvely expect geniuses-in-motion to be also geniuses-in-reflection, then their failure to be that shouldn't really seem any crueler or more disillusioning than Kant's glass jaw or Eliot's inability to hit the curve.

For my part, though, I think there's something deeper, and scarier, that keeps my hope one step ahead of past experience as I make my way to the bookstore's register. It remains very hard for me to reconcile the vapidity of Austin's narrative mind, on the one hand, with the extraordinary mental powers that are required by world-class tennis, on the other. Anyone who buys the idea that great athletes are dim should have a close look at an NFL playbook, or at a basketball coach's diagram of a 3–2 zone trap . . . or at an archival film of Ms. Tracy Austin repeatedly putting a ball in a court's corner at high speed from seventy-eight feet away, with huge sums of money at stake and enormous crowds of people watching her do it. Ever try to concentrate on doing something difficult with a crowd of people watching? . . . worse, with a crowd of spectators maybe all vocally hoping you fail so that their favorite will beat you? In my own comparatively low-level junior matches, before audiences that rarely hit three digits, it used to be all I could do to manage my sphincter. I would drive myself crazy: ". . . but what if I double-fault here and go down a break with all these folks watching? . . . don't think about it . . . yeah but except if I'm consciously not thinking about it then doesn't part of me have to think about it in order for me to remember what I'm not supposed to think about? . . . shut *up*, quit thinking about it and serve the goddamn ball . . . except how can I even be talking to myself about not thinking about it unless I'm still aware of what it is I'm talking about not thinking about?" and so on. I'd get divided, paralyzed. As most ungreat athletes do. Freeze up, choke. Lose our focus. Become self-conscious. Cease to be wholly present in our wills and choices and movements.

It is not an accident that great athletes are often called "naturals," because they can, in performance, be totally present: they can proceed on instinct and muscle-memory and autonomic will such that agent and action are one. Great athletes can do this even—and, for the truly great ones like Borg and Bird and Nicklaus and Jordan and Austin, *especially*—under wilting pressure and scrutiny. They can withstand forces of distraction that would break a mind prone to self-conscious fear in two.

The real secret behind top athletes' genius, then, may be as esoteric and obvious and dull and profound as silence itself. The real, many-veiled answer to the question of just what goes through a great player's mind as he stands at the center of hostile crowd-noise and lines up the free-throw that will decide the game might well be: *nothing at all.*

How can great athletes shut off the Iago-like voice of the self? How can they bypass the head and simply and superbly act? How, at the critical moment, can they invoke for themselves a cliché as trite as "One ball at a time" or "Gotta concentrate here," and *mean* it, and then *do* it? Maybe it's because, for top athletes, clichés present themselves not as trite but simply as true, or perhaps not even as declarative expressions with qualities like depth or triteness or falsehood or truth but as simple imperatives that are either useful or not and, if useful, to be invoked and obeyed and that's all there is to it.

What if, when Tracy Austin writes that after her 1989 car crash, "I quickly accepted that there was nothing I could do about it," the statement is not only true but *exhaustively descriptive* of the entire acceptance process she went through? Is someone stupid or shallow because she can say to herself that there's nothing she can do about something bad and so she'd better accept it, and thereupon simply accept it with no more interior struggle? Or is that person maybe somehow natively wise and profound, enlightened in the childlike way some saints and monks are enlightened?

This is, for me, the real mystery—whether such a person is an idiot or a mystic or both and/or neither. The only certainty seems to be that such a person does not produce a very good prose memoir. That plain empirical fact may be the best way to explain how Tracy Austin's actual history can be so compelling and important and her verbal account of that history not even alive. It may also, in starting to address the differences in communicability between thinking and doing and between doing and being, yield the key to why top athletes' autobiographies are at once so seductive and so disappointing for us readers. As is so often SOP with the truth, there's a cruel paradox involved. It may well be that we spectators, who are not divinely gifted as athletes, are the only ones able truly to see, articulate, and animate the experience of the gift we are denied. And that those who receive and act out the gift of athletic genius must, perforce, be blind and dumb about it—and not because blindness and dumbness are the price of the gift, but because they are its essence.

1992

Tennis Player Michael Joyce's Professional Artistry as a Paradigm of Certain Stuff about Choice, Freedom, Limitation, Joy, Grotesquerie, and Human Completeness

WHEN MICHAEL JOYCE of Los Angeles serves, when he tosses the ball and his face rises to track it, it looks like he's smiling, but he's not really smiling—his face's circumoral muscles are straining with the rest of his body to reach the ball at the top of the toss's rise. He wants to hit it fully extended and slightly out in front of him; he wants to be able to hit emphatically down on the ball, to generate enough pace to avoid an ambitious return from his opponent. Right now it's 1:00 Saturday, 22 July 1995, on the Stadium Court of the Stade Jarry tennis complex in Montreal. It's the first of the qualifying rounds for the Canadian Open, one of the major stops on the ATP's "hard-court circuit,"[1] which starts right after Wimbledon and climaxes at NYC's U.S. Open. The tossed ball rises and seems for a second to hang, waiting, cooperating, as balls always seem to do for great players. The opponent, a Canadian college star named Dan Brakus, is a very good tennis player. Michael Joyce, on the other hand, is a world-class tennis player. In 1991 he was the top-ranked junior in the United States and a finalist at Junior Wimbledon,[2] is now in his fourth year on the ATP tour, and is as of this day the 79th best tennis player on planet earth.

1. Comprising Washington, Montreal, LA, Cincinnati, Indianapolis, New Haven, and Long Island, this is possibly the most grueling part of the Association of Tennis Professionals' yearly tour, with three-digit temperatures and the cement courts shimmering like Moroccan horizons and everyone wearing a hat and even the spectators carrying sweat towels.

2. Joyce lost that final to Thomas Enqvist, now ranked in the ATP's top twenty and a potential superstar and in high-profile attendance here at Montreal.

A tacit rhetorical assumption here is that you have very probably never heard of Michael Joyce of Brentwood/LA. Nor of Florida's Tommy Ho. Nor of Vince Spadea, nor of Jonathan Stark or Robbie Weiss or Steve Bryan—all American men in their twenties, all ranked in the world's top 100 at one point in 1995. Nor of Jeff Tarango, 68th in the world, unless you remember his unfortunate psychotic break in full public view during last year's Wimbledon.[3]

You are invited to try to imagine what it would be like to be among the hundred best in the world at something. At anything. I have tried to imagine; it's hard.

Stade Jarry's Stadium Court facility can hold slightly over 10,000 souls. Right now, for Michael Joyce's qualifying match, there are 93 people in the crowd, 91 of whom appear to be friends and relatives of Dan Brakus. Michael Joyce doesn't seem to notice whether there's a crowd or not. He has a way of staring intently at the air in front of his face between points. During points he looks only at the ball.

The acoustics in the near-empty Stadium are amazing—you can hear every breath, every sneaker's squeak, the authoritative *pang* of the ball against very tight strings.

Professional tennis tournaments, like professional sports teams, have distinctive traditional colors. Wimbledon's is green; the Volvo International's is light blue. The Canadian Open's is—emphatically—red. The tournament's "title sponsor," du Maurier cigarettes,[4]

---

3. Tarango, twenty-seven, who completed three years at Stanford, is regarded as something of a scholar by Joyce and the other young Americans on tour. His little bio in the *1995 ATP Player Guide* lists his interests as including "philosophy, creative writing, and bridge," and his slight build and receding hairline do in fact make him look more like an academic or a tax attorney than a world-class tennis player. Also a native Californian, Tarango's a friend and something of a mentor to Michael Joyce, whom he practices with regularly and addresses as "Grasshopper." Joyce—who seems to like pretty much everybody—likes Jeff Tarango and won't comment on his on-court explosion at Wimbledon except to say that Tarango is "a very intense guy, very intellectual, that gets kind of paranoid sometimes."

4. Title sponsors are as important to ATP tournaments as they are to collegiate bowl games. This year the Canadian Open is officially called the "du Maurier Omnium

has ads and logos all over the place in red and black. The Stadium Court is surrounded by a red tarp festooned with corporate names in black capitals, and the tarp composes the base of a grandstand that is itself decked out in red-and-black bunting, so that from any kind of distance the place looks like either a Kremlin funeral or a really elaborate brothel. The match's umpire and linesmen and ballboys all wear black shorts and red shirts emblazoned with the name of a Quebec clothing company.[5] The big beach umbrella that's spread and held over each seated player at end-change breaks has a lush red head and a black stem that looks hot to hold.

Stade Jarry's Stadium Court is adjoined on the north by the Grandstand Court, a slightly smaller venue with seats on only one side and a capacity of 4,800. A five-story scoreboard lies just west of the Grandstand, and by late afternoon both courts are rectangularly shadowed. There are also eight nonstadium courts in canvas-fenced enclosures scattered across the grounds. Professional matches are under way on all ten Stade Jarry courts today, but they are not exactly Canadian Open matches, and for the most part they are unwatched.

Ltée." But everybody still refers to it as the Canadian Open. There are all types and levels of sponsors for big tennis tournaments—the levels of giving and of commensurate reward are somewhat similar to PBS fundraising telethons. Names of sponsors are all over the Canadian Open's site (with variations in size and placement corresponding to levels of fiscal importance to the tournament), from the big FedEx signs over the practice courts to the RADO trademark on the serve-speed radar display on the show courts. On the scarlet tarp and the box seats all around the Stadium and Grandstand Courts are the names of other corporate sponsors: TANDEM COMPUTERS/APG INC., BELL SYGMA, BANQUE LAURENTI-ENNE, IMASCO LIMITÉE, EVANS TECHNOLOGIES INC., MOBILIA, BELL CANADA, ARGO STEEL, etc.

5. Another way to be a sponsor: supply free stuff to the tournament and put your name on it in really big letters. All the courts' tall umpire-chairs have a sign that says they're supplied by TROPICANA; all the bins for fresh and unfresh towels say WAMSUTTA; the drink coolers at courtside (the size of trash barrels, with clear plastic lids) say TROPICANA and EVIAN. The players who don't individually endorse a certain brand of drink tend as a rule to drink Evian, orange juice being a bit heavy for on-court rehydration.

The Stade Jarry grounds are all spruced up, and vendors' tents are up, and Security is in place at all designated points. Big TV trailers line the walkway outside the stadium, and burly men keep pulling complicated nests of cable out of ports in the trailers' sides.

There are very few paying customers on the grounds on Saturday, but there are close to a hundred world-class players: big spidery French guys with gelled hair, American kids with peeling noses and Pac-10 sweats, lugubrious Germans, bored-looking Italians. There are blank-eyed Swedes and pockmarked Colombians and cyber-punkish Brits. There are malevolent Slavs with scary haircuts. There are Mexican players who spend their spare time playing two-on-two soccer in the gravel outside the Players' Tent. With few exceptions, all the players have similar builds: big muscular legs, shallow chests, skinny necks, and one normal-sized arm and one monstrously huge and hypertrophic arm. They tend to congregate in the Players' Tent or outside the Transportation Trailer awaiting rides in promotional BMWs back to the Radisson des Gouverneurs, the tournament's designated hotel. Many of these players in the "Qualies," or qualifying rounds, have girlfriends in tow, sloppily beautiful European girls with sandals and patched jeans and leather backpacks, girlfriends who set up cloth lawnchairs and sun themselves next to their players' practice courts.[6] At the Radisson des Gouverneurs the players tend to congregate in the lobby, where there's a drawsheet for the Qualies up on a cork bulletin board and a multilingual tournament official behind a long desk, and the players stand around in the air-conditioning in wet hair and sandals and employ about forty languages and wait for results of matches to go up on the board and for their own next matches' schedules to get posted. Some of the players listen to personal stereos; none seem to read. They all have the unhappy self-enclosed look of people who spend huge amounts of time on planes and waiting around in hotel lobbies, the look of

6. Most of the girlfriends have something indefinable about them that suggests extremely wealthy parents whom the girls are trying to piss off by hooking up with an obscure professional tennis player.   •

people who have to create an envelope of privacy around them with just their expressions. Most of these players seem either extremely young—new guys trying to break onto the Tour—or conspicuously older, like over thirty, with tans that look permanent and faces lined from years in the trenches of tennis's minor leagues.

The Canadian Open, one of the ATP Tour's "Super 9" tournaments that weigh most heavily in the calculation of world ranking, officially starts on Monday, 24 July. What's going on for the two days right before it is the Qualies. This is essentially a competition to determine who will occupy the eight slots in the Canadian Open's main draw designated for "qualifiers." It is a pre-tournament tournament. A qualifying tourney precedes just about every big-money ATP event, and money and prestige and lucrative careers are often at stake in Qualie rounds, and often they feature the best matches of the whole tournament, and it's a good bet you haven't heard of Qualies.

The realities of the men's professional tennis tour bear about as much resemblance to the lush finals you see on TV as a slaughter-house does to a well-presented cut of restaurant sirloin. For every Sampras–Agassi final we watch, there's been a week-long tournament, a pyramidical single-elimination battle among 32, 64, or 128 players, of whom the finalists are the last men standing. You probably know that already. But a player has to be eligible to enter that tournament in the first place. Eligibility is determined by ATP computer ranking. Each tournament has a cutoff, a minimum ranking required to get entered in the main draw. Players below that ranking who want to get in have to compete in a kind of pre-tournament. That's the easiest way to explain what Qualies are. In actual practice the whole thing's quite a bit messier, and I'll try to describe the logistics of the Canadian Open's Qualies in just enough detail to suggest their complexity without boring you mindless.

The du Maurier Omnium Ltée has a draw of 64. The sixteen entrants with the highest ATP rankings get "seeded," which means their names are strategically dispersed in the draw so that (barring upsets) they won't have to meet each other until the latter rounds.[7] Of the seeds, the top eight—here Agassi, Sampras, Chang, the Russian Yevgeny Kafelnikov, Croatia's Goran Ivanisevic, South Africa's Wayne Ferreira, Germany's Michael Stich, and Switzerland's Marc Rosset, respectively—get "byes," or automatic passes into the tournament's second round. This means that there is actually room for 56 players in the main draw. The cutoff for the 1995 Canadian Open isn't 56, however, because not all of the top 56 players in the world are here.[8] Here the cutoff is 85. You'd think that this meant anybody with an ATP ranking of 86 or lower would have to play the Qualies, but here too there are exceptions. The du Maurier Omnium Ltée,

---

7. The term "seeding" comes from British horticulture and is pretty straightforward. A player seeded First is expected statistically to win, Second to reach the finals, Third and Fourth the semis, etc. A player who reaches the round his seed designates is said to have "justified his seed," a term that seems far more rich in implications and entendres. Serious tennis is full of these multisemiotic terms—"love," "hold" and "break," "fault," "let" as a noun, "heat," "moon," "spank," "coming in," "playing unconscious," and so on.

8. Except for the four Grand Slams, no tournament draws all the top players, although every tournament would obviously like to, since the more top players are entered, the better the paid attendance and the more media exposure the tournament gets for itself and its sponsors. Players ranked in the world's top twenty or so, though, tend to play a comparatively light schedule of tournaments, taking time off not only for rest and training but to compete in wildly lucrative exhibitions that don't affect ATP ranking. (We're talking *wildly* lucrative, like millions of dollars per annum for the top stars.) Given the sharp divergence of interests between tournaments and players, it's not surprising that there are Kafkanly complex rules for how many ATP tournaments a player must enter each year to avoid financial or ranking-related penalties, and commensurately complex and crafty ways players have for getting around these rules and doing pretty much what they want. These will be passed over. The thing to realize is that players of Michael Joyce's station tend to take way less time off; they try to play just about every tournament they can squeeze in unless they're forced by injury or exhaustion to sit out a couple weeks. They play so much because they need to, not just financially but because the ATP's (very complex) set of algorithms for determining ranking tends to reward players for entering as many tournaments as they can.

And so even though several of the North American hard-court circuit's tournaments are Super 9's, a fair number of top players skip them, especially European clay-court players, who hate DecoTurf and tend to stick to their own summer clay-court circuit, which is European and comprises smaller and less lucrative tournaments (like the Dutch Open, which is concurrent with the Canadian and has four of the world's top twenty entered this year). The clay-courters tend to pay the price for this at the U.S. Open, which is played on hard sizzling DecoTurf courts.

like most other big tournaments, has five "wild card" entries into the main draw. These are special places given either to high-ranked players who entered after the required six-week deadline but are desirable to have in the tournament because they're big stars (like Ivanisevic, #6 in the world but a notorious flakeroo who *"forgot"* to enter till a week ago and got a last-minute wild card) or to players ranked lower than 85 whom the tournament wants because they are judged "uniquely deserving" (read "Canadian"—the other four players who get wild cards here are all Canadian, and two are Québecois).

By the way, if you're interested, the ATP Tour updates and publishes its world rankings weekly, and the rankings constitute a nomological orgy that makes for truly first-rate bathroom reading. As of this writing, Mahesh Bhupathi is 284, Luis Lobo 411. There's Martin Sinner and Guy Forget. There's Adolf Musil and Jonathan Venison and Javier Frana and Leander Paes. There's—no kidding—Cyril Suk. Rodolfo Ramos-Paganini is 337, Alex López-Móron 174. Gilad Bloom is 228 and Zoltan Nagy is 414. Names out of some postmodern Dickens: Udo Riglewski and Louis Gloria and Francisco Roig and Alexander Mronz. The 29th-best player in the world is named Slava Dosedel. There's Claude N'Goran and Han Shin (276 but falling fast) and Horacio de la Peña and Marcus Barbosa and Amos Mansdorf and Mariano Hood. Andres Zingman is currently ranked two places above Sander Groen. Horst Skoff and Kris Goossens and Thomas Hagstedt are all ranked higher than Martin Zumpft. One more reason the tournament industry sort of hates upsets is that the ATP press liaisons have to go around teaching journalists how to spell and pronounce new names.

So, skipping a whole lot more complication, the point is that eight slots in the Canadian Open's main draw are reserved for qualifiers, and the Qualies is the tournament held to determine who'll get those eight slots. The Qualies itself has a draw of 64 world-class players—the cutoff for qualifying for the Qualies is an ATP ranking of 350.[9] The Qualies won't go all the way through to the finals, only to the quarters: the eight quarterfinalists of the Qualies will receive first-round slots in the Canadian Open.[10] This means that a player in the Qualies will need to win three rounds—round of 64, round of 32, round of 16—in two days to get into the first round of the main draw.[11]

The eight seeds in the Qualies are the eight players whom the Canadian Open officials expect will make the quarters and thus get into the main draw. The top seed this weekend is Richard Krajicek,[12] a 6'5" Dutchman who wears a tiny white billed hat in the sun and rushes the net like it owes him money and in general plays like a rabid crane. Both his knees are bandaged. He's in the top twenty and hasn't had to play Qualies for years, but for this tournament he missed the entry deadline, found all the wild cards already given to uniquely deserving Canadians, and with phlegmatic Low Country cheer decided to go ahead and play the weekend Qualies for the match practice. The Qualies' second seed is Jamie Morgan, an Australian journeyman, around 100th in the world, whom Michael Joyce beat in straight sets last week in the second round of the main

9. There is here no qualifying tournament for the Qualies itself, though some particularly huge tournaments have meta-Qualies. The Qualies also have tons of wild-card berths, most of whom here are given to Canadian players, e.g. the collegian that Michael Joyce is beating up on right now in the first round.

10. These slots are usually placed right near the top seeds, which is the reason why in the televised first rounds of major tournaments you often see Agassi or Sampras smearing some totally obscure guy—that guy's usually a qualifier. It's also part of why it's so hard for somebody low-ranked enough to have to play the Qualies of tournaments to move up in the rankings enough so that he doesn't have to play Qualies anymore—he usually meets a high-ranked player in the very first round and gets smeared.

11. Which is another reason why qualifiers usually get smeared by the top players they face in the early rounds—the qualifier is playing his fourth or fifth match in three days, while the top players usually have had a couple days with their masseur and creative-visualization consultant to get ready for the first round. If asked, Michael Joyce will detail all these asymmetries and stacked odds the same way a farmer will speak of poor weather, with an absence of emotion that seems deep instead of blank.

12. (pronounced KRY-chek)

draw at the Legg Mason Tennis Classic in Washington. Michael Joyce is seeded third.

If you're wondering why Joyce, who's ranked above the #85 cutoff, is having to play the Canadian Open Qualies at all, gird yourself for one more bit of complication. The fact is that six weeks ago Joyce's ranking was *not* above the cutoff, and that's when the Canadian entry deadline was, and that's the ranking the tournament committee went on when they made up the main draw. Joyce's ranking jumped from 119 to around 80 after this year's Wimbledon, where he beat Marc Rosset (ranked 11 in the world) and reached the round of sixteen. Despite a bout of mononucleosis that kept him in bed through part of the spring, Joyce is having his best year ever as a pro and has jumped from 140 in the world to 79.[13] But he was not in the world's top 85 as of early June, and so he has to qualify in Montreal. It seems to me that Joyce, like Krajicek, might be excused for brooding darkly on the fact that four wild cards in the Canadian's main draw have been dispensed to Canadians ranked substantially lower than 85, but Joyce is stoic about it.[14]

The Qualie circuit is to professional tennis sort of what AAA baseball is to the major leagues: somebody playing the Qualies in Montreal is undeniably a world-class tennis player, but he's not quite at the level where the serious TV and money are. In the main draw of the du Maurier Omnium Ltée, a first-round loser will earn $5,400 and a second-round loser $10,300. In the Montreal Qualies, a player will receive $560 for losing in the second round and an even $0.00 for losing in the first. This might not be so bad if a lot of

---

13. At a certain point this summer his ranking will be as high as 62.

14. It turns out that a portion of the talent required to survive in the trenches of the ATP Tour is emotional: Joyce is able to keep from getting upset about stuff that struck me as hard not to get upset about. When he points out that there's "no point" getting exercised about unfairnesses you can't control, I think what he's really saying is that you either learn how not to get upset about it or you disappear from the Tour. The temperamental behavior of many of the game's top players—which gives the public the distorted idea that most pro players are oversensitive brats—is on a qualifier's view easily explainable: top players are temperamental because they can afford to be.

the entrants for the Qualies hadn't flown thousands of miles to get here. Plus there's the matter of supporting themselves in Montreal. The tournament pays the hotel and meal expenses of players in the main draw but not in the Qualies.[15] The eight survivors of the Qualies, however, will get their weekend expenses retroactively picked up by the tournament. So there's rather a lot at stake: some of the players in the Qualies are literally playing for their supper, or for the money to make airfare home or to the site of the next Qualie.

You could think of Michael Joyce's career as now kind of on the cusp between the major leagues and AAA ball. He still has to qualify for some tournaments, but more and more often he gets straight into the main draw. The move up from qualifier to main-draw player is a huge boost, both financially and psychically, but it's still a couple plateaux away from true fame and fortune. The

15. The really top players not only have their expenses comped but often get paid outright for agreeing to enter a tournament. These fees are called "guarantees" and are technically advances against prize money: in effect, an Agassi/Sampras/Becker will receive a "guarantee" of the champion's prize money (usually a couple hundred thousand) just for competing, whether he wins the tournament or not. This means that if top seed Agassi wins the Canadian Open, he wins $254,000 U.S., but if he loses, he gets the money anyway. (This is another reason why tournaments tend to hate upsets, and, some qualifiers complain, why all sorts of intangibles from match scheduling to close line-calls tend to go the stars' way.) Not all tournaments have guarantees—the Grand Slams don't, because the top players will show up for Wimbledon and the French, Australian, and U.S. Opens on their own incentive—but most have them, and the less established and prestigious a tournament, the more it needs to guarantee money to get the top players to come and attract spectators and media (which is what the tournament's title sponsor wants, very much).

Guarantees used to be against ATP rules and were under the table; they've been legal since the early '90s. There's great debate among tennis pundits about whether legal guarantees have helped the game by making the finances less shady or have hurt the game by widening the psychological gap between the stars and all the other players and by upping the pressure on tournaments to make it as likely as possible that the stars don't get upset by an unknown. It is impossible to get Michael Joyce to give a straight answer on whether he thinks guarantees are good or bad—it's not like Joyce is muddled or Nixonianly evasive about it, but rather that he can't afford to think in good/bad terms, to nurture resentment or bitterness or frustration. My guess is that he avoids these feelings because they make it even harder to play against Agassi and the rest, and he cares less about what's "right" in the grand scheme than he does about maximizing his own psychological chances against other players. This seems totally understandable, though I'm kind of awed by Joyce's evident ability to shut down lines of thinking that aren't to his advantage.

main draw's 64 or 128 players are still mostly the supporting cast for the stars we see in televised finals. But they are also the pool from which superstars are drawn. McEnroe, Sampras, and even Agassi had to play Qualies at the start of their careers, and Sampras spent a couple years losing in the early rounds of main draws before he suddenly erupted in the early '90s and started beating everybody.

Still, most main-draw players are obscure and unknown. An example is Jacob Hlasek,[16] a Czech who is working out with Switzerland's Marc Rosset on one of the practice courts this morning when I first arrive at Stade Jarry.[17] I notice them and come over to watch only because Hlasek and Rosset are so beautiful to see; at this point I have no idea who they are. They are practicing groundstrokes down the line—Rosset's forehand and Hlasek's backhand—each ball plumb-line straight and within centimeters of the corner, the players moving with the compact nonchalance I've since come to recognize in pros when they're working out: the suggestion is one of a very powerful engine in low gear. Jacob Hlasek is 6'2" and built like a halfback, his blond hair in a short square East European cut, with icy eyes and cheekbones out to here: he looks like either a Nazi male model or a lifeguard in hell and seems in general just way too scary ever to try to talk to. His backhand's a one-hander, rather like Lendl's, and watching him practice it is like watching a great artist casually sketch something. I keep having to remember to blink. There are a million little ways you can tell that somebody's a great player—details in his posture, in the way he bounces the ball with his racket-head to pick it up, in the casual way he twirls the racket while waiting for the ball. Hlasek wears a plain gray T-shirt and some kind of very white European shoes. It's midmorning and

16. (pronounced YA-kob hLA-sick)

17. It took forever to get there from the hotel because I didn't yet know that press can, with some wangling, get rides in the courtesy cars with the players, if there's room. Tennis journalism is apparently its own special world, and it takes a little while to learn the ins and outs of how media can finagle access to some of the services the tournament provides: courtesy cars, VIP treatment in terms of restaurant reservations, even free laundry service at the hotel. Most of this stuff I learned about just as I was getting ready to come home.

already at least 90° and he isn't sweating. Hlasek turned pro in 1982, six years later had one year in the top ten, and for the last decade has been ranked in the 60s and 70s, getting straight into the main draw of all the big tournaments and usually losing in the first couple rounds. Watching Hlasek practice is probably the first time it really strikes me how good these professionals are, because even just fucking around, Hlasek is the most impressive tennis player I've ever seen.[18] I'd be surprised if anybody reading this has ever heard of Jacob Hlasek. By the distorted standards of TV's obsession with Grand Slam finals and the world's top five, Hlasek is merely an also-ran. But last year he made $300,000 on the tour (that's just in prize money, not counting exhibitions and endorsement contracts), and his career winnings are over $4,000,000 U.S., and it turns out his home base for a long time was Monte Carlo, where lots of European players with tax issues end up living.

Michael Joyce is listed in the ATP Player Guide as 5'11" and 165 pounds, but in person he's more like 5'9". On the Stadium Court he looks compact and stocky. The quickest way to describe him would be to say that he looks like a young and slightly buff David Caruso. He is fair-skinned and has reddish hair and the kind of patchy, vaguely pubic goatee of somebody who isn't quite able yet to grow real facial hair. When he plays in the heat he wears a hat.[19] He wears Fila clothes and uses Yonex rackets and is paid to do so. His face is childishly full, and while it isn't freckled it somehow seems like it *ought* to be freckled. A lot of professional tennis players look like lifeguards—that kind of extreme tan that looks like it's pene-

18. Joyce is even more impressive, but I hadn't seen Joyce yet. And Enqvist is even more impressive than Joyce, and Agassi live is even more impressive than Enqvist. After the week was over, I truly understand why Charlton Heston looks gray and ravaged on his descent from Sinai: past a certain point, impressiveness is corrosive to the psyche.

19. During his two daily one-hour practice sessions he wears the hat backwards, and also wears boxy plaid shorts that look for all the world like swimtrunks. His favorite practice T-shirt has FEAR: THE ENEMY OF DREAMS on the chest. He laughs a lot when he practices. You can tell just by looking at him out there that he's totally likable and cool.

trated to the subdermal layer and will be retained to the grave—but Joyce's fair skin doesn't tan or even burn, though he does get red in the face when he plays, from effort.[20] His on-court expression is grim without being unpleasant; it communicates the sense that Joyce's attentions on-court have become very narrow and focused and intense—it's the same pleasantly grim expression you see on, say, working surgeons and jewelers. On the Stadium Court, Joyce seems boyish and extremely adult at the same time. And in contrast to the Canadian opponent, who has the varnished good looks and Pepsodent smile of the stereotypical tennis player, Joyce looks terribly *real* out there playing: he sweats through his shirt,[21] gets

20. If you've played only casually, it is probably hard to understand how physically demanding really serious tennis is. Realizing that these pros can move one another from one end of the 27' baseline to the other pretty much at will, and that they hardly ever end a point early by making an unforced error, might stimulate your imagination. A close best-of-three-set match is probably equivalent in its demands to a couple hours of basketball, but we're talking full-court basketball.

21. Something else you don't get a good sense of on television: tennis is a very sweaty game. On ESPN or whatever, when you see a player walk over to the ballboy after a point and request a towel and quickly wipe off his arm and hand and toss the wet towel back to the (rather luckless) ballboy, most of the time the towel thing isn't a stall or a meditative pause—it's because sweat is running down the inside of the player's arm in such volume that it's getting all over his hand and making the racket slippery. Especially on the sizzling North American summer junket, players sweat through their shirts early on, and sometimes also their shorts. (Sampras always wears light-blue shorts that sweat through everyplace but his jockstrap, which looks funny and kind of endearing, like he's an incontinent child—Sampras is surprisingly childlike and cute on the court, in person, in contrast to Agassi, who's about as cute as a Port Authority whore.)

And they drink enormous amounts of water, staggering amounts. I thought I was seeing things at first, watching matches, as players seemed to go through one of those skinny half-liter Evian bottles every second side-change, but Michael Joyce confirmed it. Pro-grade tennis players seem to have evolved a metabolic system that allows rapid absorption of water and its transformation into sweat. I myself—who am not pro-grade, but do sweat like a pig—drink a lot of water a couple hours before I play but don't drink anything during a match. This is because a couple swallows of water usually just makes me want more, and if I drink as much as I want I end up with a protruding tummy and a sloshing sound when I run.

(Most players I spoke with confirm, by the way, that Gatorade and All-Sport and Boost and all those pricey electrolytic sports drinks are mostly bullshit, that salt and carbs at table and small lakes of daily H_2O are the way to go. The players who didn't confirm this turned out to be players who had endorsement deals with some pricey-sports-drink manufacturer, but I personally saw at least one such player dumping out his bottle's pricey electrolytic contents and replacing them with good old water, for his match.)

flushed, whoops for breath after a long point. He wears little elastic braces on both ankles, but it turns out they're mostly prophylactic.

It's 1:30 P.M. Joyce has broken Brakus's serve once and is up 3–1 in the first set and is receiving. Brakus is in the multibrand clothes of somebody without an endorsement contract. He's well over six feet tall, and like many large male collegians his game is built around his serve.[22] At 0–15, his first serve is flat and 118 mph and way out to Joyce's backhand, which is a two-hander and hard to lunge effectively with, but Joyce lunges plenty effectively and sends the ball back down the line to the Canadian's forehand, deep in the court and with such flat pace that Brakus has to stutter-step a little and backpedal to get set up—clearly he's used to playing guys for whom 118 mumps out wide would be an outright ace or at least produce such a weak return that he could move up easily and put the ball away—and Brakus now sends the ball back up the line high over the net, loopy with topspin, not all that bad a shot considering the fierceness of the return, and a topspin shot that'd back most tennis players up and put them on the defensive, but Michael Joyce, whose level of tennis is such that he moves *in* on balls hit with topspin and hits them on the rise,[23] moves in and takes the ball on the rise and hits a backhand cross so tightly angled that nobody alive could get to it. This is kind of a typical Joyce–Brakus point. The match is carnage of a particular high-level sort: it's like watching an extremely large and powerful predator get torn to pieces by an even larger and more powerful predator. Brakus looks pissed off after Joyce's winner, makes some berating-himself-type noises, but the anger

22. The taller you are, the harder you can serve (get a protractor and figure it out), but the less able to bend and reverse direction you are. Tall guys tend to be serve-and-volleyers, and they live and die by their serves. Bill Tilden, Stan Smith, Arthur Ashe, Roscoe Tanner, and Goran Ivanisevic were/are all tall guys with serve-dependent games.

23. This is mind-bogglingly hard to do when the ball's hit hard. If we can assume you've played Little League or sandlot ball or something, imagine the hardest-hit grounder of all time coming at you at shortstop, and then you not standing waiting to try to knock it down but actually of your own free will running forward *toward* the grounder, then trying not just to catch it in a big soft glove but to strike it hard and reverse its direction and send it someplace frightfully specific and far away.

seems kind of pro forma: it's not like there's anything Brakus could have done much better, not given what he and the 79th-best player in the world have in their respective arsenals.

Michael Joyce—whose realness and approachability and candor are a big reason why he's whom I end up spending the most time watching and talking to—will later say, in response to my dry observation that a rather disproportionate number of unranked Canadians seem to have gotten wild cards into the Montreal Qualies, that Brakus "had a big serve, but the guy didn't belong on a pro court." Joyce didn't mean this in an unkind way. Nor did he mean it in a kind way. It turns out that what Michael Joyce says rarely has any kind of spin or slant on it; he mostly just reports what he sees, rather like a camera. You couldn't even call him sincere, because it's not like it seems ever to occur to him to *try* to be sincere or nonsincere. For a while I thought that Joyce's rather bland candor was a function of his not being very bright. This judgment was partly informed by the fact that Joyce didn't go to college and was only marginally involved in his high school academics (stuff I know because he told me it right away).[24] What I discovered as

---

24. Something else that's hotly debated by tennis authorities is the trend of players going pro at younger and younger ages and skipping college and college tennis and plunging into the stress and peripatetic loneliness of the Tour, etc. Michael Joyce skipped college and went directly onto the pro tour because at eighteen he'd just won the U.S. National Juniors, and this created a set of overwhelming inducements to turn pro. The winner at the National 18-and-Under Singles automatically gets a wild card into the U.S. Open's main draw for that year. In addition, a year's top junior comes to the powerful but notoriously fickle and temporary attention of major clothing and racket companies. Joyce's victory over the 128-man National field at Kalamazoo MI in 1991 resulted in endorsement offers from Fila and Yonex worth around $100,000. $100,000 is about what it takes to finance three years on the Tour for a very young player who can't reasonably expect to earn a whole lot of prize-money.

Joyce could have turned down that offer of a three-year subsidy and gone to college, but if he'd gone to college it would have been primarily to play tennis. Coaches at major universities apparently offered Joyce inducements to come play for them so literally outrageous and incredible that I wouldn't repeat them here even if Joyce hadn't asked me not to.

The reason why Michael Joyce would have gone to college primarily to play tennis is that the academic and social aspects of collegiate life interest him about as much as hitting 2,500 crosscourt forehands while a coach yells at you in foreign

the tournament wore on was that I can be kind of a snob and an asshole, and that Michael Joyce's affectless openness is a sign not of stupidity but of something else.

Advances in racket technology and conditioning methods over the last decade have dramatically altered men's professional tennis. For much of the twentieth century, there were two basic styles of top-level play. The "offensive"[25] style is based on the serve and

---

languages would interest you. Tennis is what Michael Joyce loves and lives for and *is*. He sees little point in telling anybody anything different. It's the only thing he's devoted himself to, and he's given massive amounts of himself to it, and as far as he understands it it's all he wants to do or be. Because he started playing at age two and competing at age seven, however, and had the first half-dozen years of his career directed rather shall we say *forcefully* and *enthusiastically* by his father (who Joyce estimates spent probably around $250,000 on lessons and court-time and equipment and travel during Michael's junior career), it seemed reasonable to ask Joyce to what extent he "*chose*" to devote himself to tennis. Can you "*choose*" something when you are forcefully and enthusiastically immersed in it at an age when the resources and information necessary for choosing are not yet yours?

Joyce's response to this line of inquiry strikes me as both unsatisfactory and marvelous. Because of course the question is unanswerable, at least it's unanswerable by a person who's already—as far as he understands it—"*chosen*." Joyce's answer is that it doesn't really matter much to him whether he originally "*chose*" serious tennis or not; all he knows is that he loves it. He tries to explain his feelings at the Nationals in 1991: "You get there and look at the draw, it's a 128 draw, there's so many guys you have to beat. And then it's all over and you've won, you're the National Champion—there's nothing like it. I get chills even talking about it." Or how it was just the previous week in Washington: "I'm playing Agassi, and it's great tennis, and there's like thousands of fans going nuts. I can't describe the feeling. Where else could I get that?"

What he says aloud is understandable, but it's not the marvelous part. The marvelous part is the way Joyce's face looks when he talks about what tennis means to him. He loves it; you can see this in his face when he talks about it: his eyes normally have a kind of Asiatic cast because of the slight epicanthic fold common to ethnic Irishmen, but when he speaks of tennis and his career the eyes get round and the pupils dilate and the look in them is one of love. The love is not the love one feels for a job or a lover or any of the loci of intensity that most of us choose to say we love. It's the sort of love you see in the eyes of really old people who've been happily married for an incredibly long time, or in religious people who are so religious they've devoted their lives to religious stuff: it's the sort of love whose measure is what it has cost, what one's given up for it. Whether there's "*choice*" involved is, at a certain point, of no interest . . . since it's the very surrender of choice and self that informs the love in the first place.

25. (aka serve-and-volley; see Note 22)

the net game and is ideally suited to slick (or "fast") surfaces like grass and cement. The "defensive" or "baseline" style is built around foot-speed, consistency, and groundstrokes accurate enough to hit effective passing shots against a serve-and-volleyer; this style is most effective on "slow" surfaces like clay and Har-Tru composite. John McEnroe and Björn Borg are probably the modern era's greatest exponents of the offensive and defensive styles, respectively.

There is now a third way to play, and it tends to be called the "power-baseline" style. As far as I can determine, Jimmy Connors[26] more or less invented the power-baseline game back in the '70s, and in the '80s Ivan Lendl raised it to a kind of brutal art. In the '90s, the majority of young players on the ATP Tour now have a P.B.-type game. This game's cornerstone is groundstrokes, but groundstrokes hit with incredible pace, such that winners from the baseline are not unusual.[27] A power-baseliner's net game tends to be solid but uninspired—a P.B.er is more apt to hit a winner on the approach shot and not need to volley at all. His serve is competent and reasonably forceful, but the really inspired part of a P.B.er's game is

---

26. I don't know whether you know this, but Connors had one of the most eccentric games in the history of tennis—he was an aggressive "power" player who rarely came to net, had the serve of an ectomorphic girl, and hit everything totally spinless and flat (which is inadvisable on groundstrokes because the absence of spin makes the ball so hard to control). His game was all the stranger because the racket he generated all his firepower from the baseline with was a Wilson T2000, a weird steel thing that's one of the single shittiest tennis rackets ever made and is regarded by most serious players as useful only for home defense or prying large rocks out of your backyard or something. Connors was addicted to this racket and kept using it even after Wilson stopped making it, forfeiting millions in potential endorsement money by doing so. Connors was eccentric (and kind of repulsive) in lots of other ways, too, none of which are germane to this article.

27. In the yore days before wide-body ceramic rackets and scientific strength-training, the only two venues for hitting winners used to be the volley—where your decreased distance from the net allowed for greatly increased angle (get that protractor out)—and the defensive passing shot . . . i.e., in the tactical language of boxing, "punch" vs. "counterpunch." The new power-baseline game allows a player, in effect, to punch his opponent all the way from his stool in the corner; it changes absolutely everything, and the analytic geometry of these changes would look like the worst calculus final you ever had in your life.

usually his return of serve.[28] He usually has incredible reflexes and can hit winners right off the return. The P.B.er's game requires both the power and aggression of an offensive style and the speed and calculated patience of a defensive style. It is adjustable both to slick grass and to slow clay, but its most congenial surface is DecoTurf,[29] the type of slow abrasive hard-court surface now used at the U.S. Open and at all the broiling North American tournaments leading up to it, including the Canadian Open.

Boris Becker and Stefan Edberg are contemporary examples of the classic offensive style. Serve-and-volleyers are often tall,[30] and tall Americans like Pete Sampras and Todd Martin and David Wheaton are also offensive players. Michael Chang is an exponent of the pure defensive style, as are Mats Wilander, Carlos Costa, and a lot of the Tour's Western Europeans and South Americans, many of whom grew up exclusively on clay and now stick primarily to the overseas clay-court circuits. Americans Jim Courier, Jimmy Arias, and Aaron Krickstein all play a power-baseline game. So does just about every young new male player on the Tour. But the style's most famous and effective post-Lendl avatar is Andre Agassi, who on 1995's summer circuit is simply kicking everyone's ass.[31]

28. This is why the phenomenon of "breaking serve" in a set is so much less important when a match involves power-baseliners. It is one reason why so many older players and fans no longer like to watch pro tennis as much: the structural tactics of the game are now wholly different from when they played.

29. © Wichita KS's Koch Materials Company, "A Leader in Asphalt-Emulsions Technology."

30. John McEnroe wasn't all that tall, and he was arguably the best serve-and-volley man of all time, but then McEnroe was an exception to pretty much every predictive norm there was. At his peak (say 1980 to 1984), he was the greatest tennis player who ever lived—the most talented, the most beautiful, the most tormented: a genius. For me, watching McEnroe don a polyester blazer and do stiff lame truistic color commentary for TV is like watching Faulkner do a Gap ad.

31. One answer to why public interest in men's tennis has been on the wane in recent years is an essential and unpretty *thuggishness* about the power-baseline style that's come to dominate the Tour. Watch Agassi closely sometime—for so small a man and so great a player, he's amazingly devoid of finesse, with movements that look more like a Heavy Metal musician's than an athlete's.

The power-baseline game itself has been compared to Metal or Grunge. But

Michael Joyce's style is power-baseline in the Agassi mold: Joyce is short and right-handed and has a two-handed backhand, a serve that's just good enough to set up the baseline attack, and a great return of serve that's the linchpin of his game. Like Agassi, Joyce takes the ball early, on the rise, so it always looks like he's moving forward in the court even though he rarely comes to net. Joyce's first serve usually comes in around 95 mph,[32] and his second serve is in the low 80s, but it has so much spin on it that the ball turns weird shapes in the air and bounces high and wide to the first-round Canadian's backhand. Brakus stretches for the ball and floats a slice return, the sort of weak return that a serve-and-volleyer'd be rushing up to the net to put away on the fly. Joyce does move up, but only to midcourt, right around his own service line, where he lets the floater land and bounce up all ripe, and he winds up his forehand and hits a winner crosscourt into the deuce corner, very flat and hard, so that the ball makes an emphatic sound as it hits the scarlet tarp behind Brakus's end of the court. Ballboys move for the ball and reconfigure complexly as Joyce walks back to serve another point. The applause of the tiny crowd is so small and sad and shabby-sounding that it'd almost be better if people didn't clap at all.

As with Lendl and Agassi and Courier and many P.B.ers, Joyce's strongest shot is his forehand, a weapon of near-Wagnerian aggression and power. Joyce's forehand is particularly lovely to watch. It's more spare and textbook than Lendl's whip-crack forehand or Borg's great swooping loop; by way of decoration there's only a small loop of flourish[33] on the backswing. The stroke itself is com-

---

what a top P.B.er really resembles is film of the old Soviet Union putting down a rebellion. It's awesome, but brutally so, with a grinding, faceless quality about its power that renders that power curiously dull and empty.

32. (compare Ivanisevic's at 130 mph or Sampras's at 125, or even this Brakus kid's at 118)

33. The loop in a pro's backswing is kind of the trademark flourish of excellence and consciousness of same, not unlike the five-star chef's quick kiss of his own fingertips as he presents a pièce or the magician's hand making a French curl in the air as he directs our attention to his vanished assistant.

pletely horizontal, so Joyce can hit through the ball while it's still well out in front of him. As with all great players, Joyce's side is so emphatically to the net as the ball approaches that his posture is a classic contrapposto.

As Joyce on the forehand makes contact with the tennis ball, his left hand behind him opens up, as if he were releasing something, a decorative gesture that has nothing to do with the mechanics of the stroke. Michael Joyce doesn't know that his left hand opens up at impact on forehands: it is unconscious, some aesthetic tic that started when he was a child and is now inextricably hardwired into a stroke that is itself unconscious for Joyce, now, at twenty-two, after years of hitting more forehands over and over than anyone could ever count.[34]

Agassi, who is twenty-five (and of whom you have heard and then some), is kind of Michael Joyce's hero. Just last week, at the Legg Mason Tennis Classic in Washington D.C., in wet-mitten heat that had players vomiting on-court and defaulting all over the place, Agassi beat Joyce in the third round of the main draw, 6–2 6–2. Every once in a while now during this Qualie match Joyce will look over at his coach next to me in the player-guest section of the Grandstand and grin and say something like "Agassi'd have killed me on that shot." Joyce's coach will adjust the set of his sunglasses and say nothing—coaches are forbidden to say anything to their

34. All serious players have these little extraneous tics, stylistic fingerprints, and the pros even more so because of years of repetition and ingraining. Pros' tics have always been fun to note and chart, even just e.g. on the serve. Watch the way Sampras's lead foot rises from the heel on his toss, as if his left foot's toes got suddenly hot. The odd Tourettic way Gerulaitis used to whip his head from side to side while bouncing the ball before his toss, as if he were having a small seizure. McEnroe's weird splayed stiff-armed service stance, both feet parallel to the baseline and his side so severely to the net that he looked like a figure on an Egyptian frieze. The odd sudden shrug Lendl gives before releasing his toss. The way Agassi shifts his weight several times from foot to foot as he prepares for the toss like he needs desperately to pee. Or, here at the Canadian Open, the way the young star Thomas Enqvist's body bends queerly back as he tosses, limboing back away from the toss, as if for a moment the ball smelled very bad—this tic derives from Enqvist's predecessor Edberg's own weird spinal arch and twist on the toss. Edberg also has this strange sudden way of switching his hold on the racket in mid-toss, changing from an Eastern forehand to an extreme backhand grip, as if the racket were a skillet.

players during a match. Joyce's coach, Sam Aparicio,[35] a protégé of Pancho Gonzalez, is based in Las Vegas, which is also Agassi's home town, and Joyce has several times been flown to Las Vegas at Agassi's request to practice with him, and is apparently regarded by Agassi as a friend and peer—these are facts Michael Joyce will mention with as much pride as he evinces in speaking of victories and world ranking.

There are big differences between Agassi's and Joyce's games, though. Though Joyce and Agassi both use the Western forehand grip and two-handed backhand that are distinctive of topspinners, Joyce's groundstrokes are very "flat"—i.e. spinless, passing low over the net, driven rather than brushed—because the actual motion of his strokes is so levelly horizontal. Joyce's balls actually look more like Jimmy Connors's balls than like Agassi's.[36] Some of Joyce's

---

35. Who looks rather like a Hispanic Dustin Hoffman and is an almost unbelievably nice guy, with the sort of inward self-sufficiency of truly great teachers and coaches everywhere, the Zen-like blend of focus and calm developed by people who have to spend enormous amounts of time sitting in one place watching closely while somebody else does something. Sam gets 10% of Joyce's gross revenues and spends his downtime reading dense tomes on Mayan architecture and is one of the coolest people I've ever met either inside the tennis world or outside it (so cool I'm kind of scared of him and haven't called him once since the assignment ended, if that makes sense). In return for his 10%, Sam travels with Joyce, rooms with him, coaches him, supervises his training, analyzes his matches, and attends him in practice, even to the extent of picking up errant balls so that Joyce doesn't have to spend any of his tightly organized practice time picking up errant balls. The stress and weird loneliness of pro tennis—where everybody's in the same community, sees each other every week, but is constantly on the diasporic move, and is each other's rival, with enormous amounts of money at stake and life essentially a montage of airports and bland hotels and non-home-cooked food and nagging injuries and staggering long-distance bills, and people's families back home tending to be wackos, since only wackos will make the financial and temporal sacrifices necessary to let their offspring become good enough at something to turn pro at it—all this means that most players lean heavily on their coaches for emotional support and friendship as well as technical counsel. Sam's role with Joyce looks to me to approximate what in the latter century was called that of "companion," one of those older ladies who traveled with nubile women when they went abroad, etc.

36. Agassi's balls look more like Borg's balls would have looked if Borg had been on a year-long regimen of both steroids and methamphetamines and was hitting every single fucking ball just as hard as he could—Agassi hits his groundstrokes as hard as anybody who's ever played tennis, so hard you almost can't believe it if you're right there by the court.

groundstrokes look like knuckleballs going over the net, and you can actually see the ball's seams just hanging there, not spinning. Joyce also has a hitch in his backhand that makes it look stiff and slightly awkward, though his pace and placement are lethal off that side; Agassi's own backhand is flowing and hitchless.[37] And while Joyce is far from slow, he lacks Agassi's otherworldly foot-speed. Agassi is every bit as fast as Michael Chang, and watch A.A. on TV sometime as he's walking between points: he takes these tiny, violently pigeon-toed steps, the stride of a man whose feet weigh basically nothing.

Michael Joyce also—in his own coach's opinion—doesn't "see" the ball in the same magical way that Andre Agassi does, and so Joyce can't take the ball as early or generate quite the same amount of pace off his groundstrokes. This business of "seeing" is important enough to explain. Except for the serve, power in tennis is a matter not of strength but of timing. This is one reason why so few top tennis players are muscular.[38] Any normal adult male can hit a tennis ball with pro pace; the trick is being able to hit the ball both hard and accurately. If you can get your body in just the right position and time your stroke so you hit the ball in just the right spot—waist-level, just slightly out in front of you, with your weight moving from your back leg to your front leg as you make contact—you can both cream the ball and direct it. And since ". . . just the

37. But Agassi does have this exaggerated follow-through where he keeps both hands on the racket and follows through almost like a hitter in baseball, which causes his shirtfront to lift and his hairy tummy to be exposed to public view—in Montreal I find this repellent, though the females in the stands around me seem ready to live and die for a glimpse of Agassi's tummy. Agassi's S.O. Brooke Shields is in Montreal, by the way, and will end up highly visible in the player-guest box for all Agassi's matches, wearing big sunglasses and what look to be multiple hats. This may be the place to insert that Brooke Shields is rather a lot taller than Agassi, and considerably less hairy, and that seeing them standing together in person is rather like seeing Sigourney Weaver on the arm of Danny DeVito. The effect is especially surreal when Brooke is wearing one of the plain classy sundresses that make her look like a deb summering in the Hamptons and Agassi's wearing his new Nike on-court ensemble, a blue-black horizontally striped outfit that together with his black sneakers makes him look like somebody's idea of a French Resistance fighter.

38. (Though note that very few of them wear eyeglasses, either.)

right . . ." is a matter of millimeters and microseconds, a certain kind of vision is crucial.[39] Agassi's vision is literally one in a billion, and it allows him to hit his groundstrokes as hard as he can just about every time. Joyce, whose hand-eye coordination is superlative, in the top 1% of all athletes everywhere (he's been exhaustively tested), still has to take some incremental bit of steam off most of his groundstrokes if he wants to direct them.

I submit that tennis is the most beautiful sport there is,[40] and also the most demanding. It requires body control, hand-eye coordination, quickness, flat-out speed, endurance, and that strange mix of caution and abandon we call courage. It also requires smarts. Just one single shot in one exchange in one point of a high-level match is a nightmare of mechanical variables. Given a net that's three feet high (at the center) and two players in (unrealistically) a fixed position, the efficacy of one single shot is determined by its angle, depth, pace, and spin. And each of these determinants is itself determined by still other variables—for example, a shot's depth is determined by the height at which the ball passes over the net combined with some integrated function of pace and spin, with the ball's height over the net *itself* determined by the player's body position, grip on the racket, degree of backswing, angle of racket face, and the 3-D coordinates through which the racket face moves during that interval in which the ball is actually on the strings. The tree of variables and determinants branches out, on and on, and then on even farther when the opponent's own positions and predilections and

39. A whole other kind of vision—the kind attributed to Larry Bird in basketball, sometimes, when he made those incredible surgical passes to people who nobody else could even see were open—is required when you're hitting: this involves seeing the other side of the court, i.e. where your opponent is and which direction he's moving in and what possible angles are open to you in consequence of where he's going. The schizoid thing about tennis is that you have to use both kinds of vision— ball and court—at the same time.

40. Basketball comes close, but it's a team sport and lacks tennis's primal mano a mano intensity. Boxing might come close—at least at the lighter weight-divisions— but the actual physical damage the fighters inflict on each other makes it too concretely brutal to be really beautiful: a level of abstraction and formality (i.e. "play") is probably necessary for a sport to possess true metaphysical beauty (in my opinion).

the ballistic features of the ball he's sent you to hit are factored in.[41] No CPU yet existent could compute the expansion of variables for even a single exchange—smoke would come out of the mainframe. The sort of thinking involved is the sort that can be done only by a living and highly conscious entity, and then only *un*consciously, i.e. by combining talent with repetition to such an extent that the variables are combined and controlled without conscious thought. In other words, serious tennis is a kind of art.

If you've played tennis at least a little, you probably think you have some idea of how hard a game it is to play really well. I submit to you that you really have no idea at all. I know I didn't. And television doesn't really allow us to appreciate what real top-level players can do—how hard they're actually hitting the ball, and with what control and tactical imagination and artistry. I got to watch Michael Joyce practice several times, right up close, like six feet and a chain-link fence away. This is a man who, at full run, can hit a fast-moving tennis ball into a one-foot-square area 78 feet away over a yard-high net, hard. He can do this something over 90% of the time. And this is the world's 79th-best player, one who has to play the Montreal Qualies.

It's not just the athletic artistry that compels interest in tennis at the professional level. It's also what this level requires—what it's taken for the 100th-ranked player in the world to get there, what it takes to stay, what it would take to rise even higher against other men who've paid the same price he's paid.

Bismarck's epigram about diplomacy and sausage applies also to the way we Americans seem to feel about professional athletes. We revere athletic excellence, competitive success. And it's more than attention we pay; we vote with our wallets. We'll spend large sums

---

41. For those of you into business stats, the calculus of a shot in tennis would be rather like establishing a running compound-interest expansion in a case where not only is the rate of interest itself variable, and not only are the determinants of that rate variable, and not only is the interval in which the determinants influence the interest rate variable, but the principal *itself* is variable.

to watch a truly great athlete; we'll reward him with celebrity and adulation and will even go so far as to buy products and services he endorses.

But we prefer not to countenance the kinds of sacrifices the professional-grade athlete has made to get so good at one particular thing. Oh, we'll pay lip service to these sacrifices—we'll invoke lush clichés about the lonely heroism of Olympic athletes, the pain and analgesia of football, the early rising and hours of practice and restricted diets, the privations, the prefight celibacy, etc. But the actual facts of the sacrifices repel us when we see them: basketball geniuses who cannot read, sprinters who dope themselves, defensive tackles who shoot up bovine hormones until they collapse or explode. We prefer not to consider the shockingly vapid and primitive comments uttered by athletes in postcontest interviews, or to imagine what impoverishments in one's mental life would allow people actually to think in the simplistic way great athletes seem to think. Note the way "up-close and personal profiles" of professional athletes strain so hard to find evidence of a rounded human life—outside interests and activities, charities, values beyond the sport. We ignore what's obvious, that most of this straining is farce. It's farce because the realities of top-level athletics today require an early and total commitment to one pursuit. An almost ascetic focus.[42] A subsumption of almost all other features of human life to their one chosen talent and pursuit. A consent to live in a world that, like a child's world, is very serious and very small.

Playing two professional singles matches on the same day is unheard of, except in Qualies.[43] Michael Joyce's second qualifying

42. Sex- and substance-issues notwithstanding, professional athletes are in many ways our culture's holy men: they give themselves over to a pursuit, endure great privation and pain to actualize themselves at it, and enjoy a relationship to perfection that we admire and reward (the monk's begging bowl, the RBI-guru's eight-figure contract) and love to watch even though we have no inclination to walk that road ourselves. In other words they do it "for" us, sacrifice themselves for our (we imagine) redemption.

43. In the Qualies for Grand Slams like Wimbledon and the U.S. Open, players

round is at 7:30 Saturday night. He's playing an Austrian named Julian Knowle, a tall and cadaverous guy with pointy Kafkan ears. Knowle uses two hands off both sides[44] and throws his racket when he's mad. The match takes place on Stade Jarry's Grandstand Court, which seems more like a theater than an arena because it has seats and bleachers only on the east side. But the Grandstand's also more intimate: the box seats start just a few yards from the court surface, and you're close enough to see a wen on Joyce's cheek or the abacus of sweat on Herr Knowle's forehead. It's not as hot here at night, but it's humid, and the high-power lights all have those curious rainbow globes of diffraction around them, plus orbiting bugs. The Grandstand can hold maybe 1,500 people, and tonight there are exactly four human beings in the audience as Michael Joyce basically beats the everliving shit out of Julian Knowle, who will be at the Montreal airport tonight at 1:30 to board the red-eye for a kind of minor-league clay tournament in Poznan, Poland.

During this afternoon's match Joyce wore a white Fila shirt with two different-colored sleeves. Onto his sleeve was sewn a patch that says POWERBAR; Joyce is paid $1,000 each time he wears this patch in play. Plus, this afternoon, a hat—in the afternoon sun, pretty much all the players in the Qualies wear hats. For tonight's match Joyce wears a pinstripe Jim Courier–model Fila shirt with one red sleeve and one blue sleeve. The patch is on the blue sleeve. He has a red bandanna around his head, and as he begins to perspire in the humidity his face turns the same color as the bandanna. It is hard not to find this endearing. Julian Knowle has an abstract pastel shirt whose brand is unrecognizable. He has very tall hair, Knowle does, that towers over his head at near-Beavis altitude and doesn't

---

sometimes have to play two three-out-of-five-set matches in one day; it is little wonder that the surviving qualifiers often look like concentration-camp survivors by the time they get to the main draw and you see them getting annihilated by a healthy and rested top seed in the televised first round.

44. Meaning a two-handed forehand, whose pioneer was a South African named Frew McMillan and whose most famous practitioner today is Monica Seles.

diminish or lose its gelled integrity as he perspires.[45] Knowle's shirt, too, has sleeves of different colors. This seems to be the fashion constant this year among the qualifiers: sleeve-color asymmetry.

The Joyce–Knowle match takes slightly more than an hour. This is including delays caused when Knowle throws his racket and has to go retrieve it or when he walks around in aimless circles muttering blackly to himself in some High German dialect. Knowle's tantrums seem a little contrived and insincere to me, though, because he rarely loses a point as a result of doing anything particularly wrong. Here's a typical point in this match: it's 1–4 and 15–30 in the sixth game. Knowle hits a 110-mph slice serve to Joyce's forehand; Joyce hits a very flat and penetrating drive crosscourt, so that Knowle has to stretch and hit his forehand on the run, something that's not particularly easy to do with a two-handed forehand. Knowle gets to the forehand and hits a thoroughly respectable shot, loopy with topspin and landing maybe only a little bit short, a few feet behind the service line, whereupon he reverses direction and starts scrambling back to get in the middle of the baseline to get ready for his next shot. Joyce, as is SOP, has moved in on the slightly short ball and takes the ball on the rise just after it's bounced, driving a backhand even flatter and harder into the exact same place he hit his last shot, the spot Knowle is scrambling away from. Knowle is now forced to reverse direction and get back to where he was.[46] This he does, and he gets his racket on the ball, but only barely, and sends back a weak little USDA Prime loblet that Joyce, now in the actual vicinity of the net, has little trouble blocking into the open court for a winner. The four people clap, Knowle's racket goes spinning into the blood-colored tarp, and Joyce walks expressionlessly

---

45. The idea of what it would be like to perspire heavily with large amounts of gel in your hair is sufficiently horrific to me that I approached Knowle after the match to ask him about it, only to discover that neither he nor his coach spoke enough English or even French to be able to determine who I was, and the whole sweat-and-gel issue will, I'm afraid, remain a matter for your own imagination.

46. What Joyce has done is known as "wrong-footing" his opponent, though the intransigent Francophone press here keep calling the tactic a "contre-pied."

back to the deuce court to receive again whenever Knowle gets around to serving. Knowle has slightly more firepower than the first round's Brakus: his groundstrokes are formidable, probably even lethal if he has sufficient time to get to the ball and get set up. Joyce simply denies him that time. Joyce will later admit that he wasn't working all that hard in this match, and he doesn't need to. He hits few spectacular winners, but he also makes very few unforced errors, and his shots are designed to make the somewhat clumsy Knowle move a lot and to deny him the time and the peace ever to set up his game. This strategy is one that Knowle cannot solve or interdict: he hasn't got the tools for it. This may be one reason why Joyce is unaffronted by having to play the Qualies for Montreal: barring some kind of injury or neurological dysfunction, he's not going to lose to somebody like Austria's Julian Knowle—Joyce is simply on a different plateau from the mass of these Qualie players.

The idea that there can be wholly distinct levels to competitive tennis—levels so distinct that what's being played is in essence a whole different game—might seem to you weird and hyperbolic. I have played probably just enough tennis to understand that it's true. I have played against men who were on a whole different, higher plateau than I, and I have understood on the deepest and most humbling level the impossibility of beating them, of "solving their game." Knowle is technically entitled to be called a professional, but he is playing a fundamentally different grade of tennis from Michael Joyce's, one constrained by limitations Joyce does not have. I feel like I could get on a tennis court with Julian Knowle. He would beat me, perhaps badly, but I don't feel like it would be absurd for me to occupy the same 78' × 27' rectangle as he. But the idea of me playing Joyce—or even hitting around with him, which was one of the ideas I was entertaining on the flight to Montreal, to hit around with a hot young U.S. pro—is now revealed to me to be absurd and in a certain way obscene, and during this night match I resolve not even to let Joyce[47] know that I used to play competitive

47. Who is clearly such a fundamentally nice guy that he would probably hit around

tennis, to play seriously and (I'd presumed) rather well. This makes me sad.

Sunday, the second day of the Qualies, is mostly a rainout. It rains off and on all day. The umpire, courtside in his tall chair, decides when the rain's falling hard enough to suspend play. A second-round match between the world's 219th- and 345th-ranked players gets suspended four different times and takes most of the day to complete. What happens when it rains is reminiscent of baseball. The players are hustled off back to the Players' Tent but can't leave because it could stop raining any minute; they have to just sit there, match-ready. The spectators (there are slightly more on the second day) stay where they are, but little fungal domes of umbrella start appearing all over the stands. The local Quebec reporters up in the Press Box curse in French and bring out newspapers or hand-held video games or begin telling one another long sexual-adventure stories that my French is just good enough to establish as tiresome.

When it stops raining and stays stopped long enough for the umpire to give the old raised thumb, there's suddenly a flurry of custodial activity down on the Stadium Court, a Chinese fire drill of ballboys and linesmen turned groundskeepers. Strange and expensive-looking machinery appears from nowhere and is brought to bear: huge riding-mowerish forced-air machines go over the court, bludgeoning the pooled rainwater and spreading it out; then a platoon of squeegees goes over every centimeter of the surface; then portable blowers—rather like leaf-blowers, with an over-the-shoulder strap and a wand attachment—are applied to the persistent individual wet spots that always beset a drying court.

This article is about Michael Joyce and the untelevised realities of the Tour, not me. But since a big part of my experience of the Canadian Open and its players was one of sadness, it might be worth-

---

with me for a little while just out of politeness, since for him it would be at worst somewhat dull. For me, though, it would be obscene.

while to spend a little time letting you know where I'm coming from w/r/t these players. As a young person I played competitive tennis, traveling to tournaments all over the Midwest. Most of my best friends were also tennis players, and on a regional level we were fairly successful, and we thought of ourselves as extremely good players. Tennis and our proficiency at it were tremendously important to us—a serious junior gives up a lot of his time and freedom to develop his game,[48] and it can very easily come to constitute a big part of his identity and self-worth. The other fourteen-year-old Midwest hotshots and I knew that our fishpond was somehow limited; we knew that there was a national level of play and that there existed hotshots and champions at that level. But levels and plateaus beyond our own seemed abstract, somehow unreal— those of us who were the hotshots in our region literally could not imagine players our own age who were substantially better than we.

A child's world turns out to be very small. If I'd been just a little bit better, an actual regional champion, I would have qualified for national-level tournaments, and I would have gotten to see that there were fourteen-year-olds in the United States who were playing tennis on a level I knew nothing about.

My own game as a junior was a particular type of the classic defensive style, a strategy Martin Amis describes as "craven retrieval." I didn't hit the ball all that hard, but I rarely made unforced errors,

---

48. The example of Michael Joyce's own childhood, though, shows that my friends and I were comparative sluggards, dilettantes. He describes his daily schedule thusly: "I'd be in school till 2:00. Then, after, I'd go [driven by father] to the [West End Tennis] Club [in Torrance CA] and have a lesson with [legendary, wildly expensive, and unbelievably hard-ass Robert] Lansdorp [former childhood coach of, among others, Tracy Austin] from 3:00 to 4:00. Then I'd have drills from 4:00 to 6:00, then we'd drive all the way home—it's like half an hour—and I'm like, 'Thank God, I can watch TV or go up and talk with [friends] on the phone or something,' but Dad is like, 'You didn't practice your serve yet.' At twelve or thirteen [years old], you're not going to want to do it. [No lie, since two hours of serious drills alone were usually enough to put your correspondent in a fetal position for the rest of the day.] You need somebody to make you do it. [This is one way of looking at it.] But then, after like a hundred or so serves, I start to get into it [standing by himself out on the Joyces' tennis court in their backyard with a huge bucket of balls and hitting serve after serve to no one in what must by then have been the gathering twilight], I like it, I'm glad I'm doing it."

and I was fast, and my general approach was simply to keep hitting the ball back to the opponent until the kid screwed up and either made an unforced error or hit a ball so short and juicy that even I could hit a winner off it. It doesn't look like a very glamorous or even interesting way to play, now that I see it here in bald retrospective print, but it was interesting to me, and you'd be surprised how effective it was (on the level at which I was competing, at least). At age twelve, a good competitive player will still generally miss after four or five balls (mostly because he'll get impatient or grandiose). At age sixteen, a good player will keep the ball in play for more like maybe seven or eight shots before he misses. At the collegiate level, too (at least in Division III), opponents were stronger than junior players but not markedly more consistent, and if I could keep a rally going to seven or eight shots, I could usually win the point on the other guy's mistake.[49]

49. An important variable I'm skipping is that children are (not surprisingly) immature and tend to get angry with themselves when they screw up, and so a key part of my strategy involved putting the opponent in a position where he made a lot of unforced errors and got madder and madder at himself, which would ruin his game. Feelings of self-disgust at his errors, or (even better for me) bitter grievance at the universe for making him have "bad luck" or an "off day" would mount until usually by sometime in the second set he'd sink into a kind of enraged torpor and *expect* to miss, or occasionally he'd even have a kind of grand Learesque tantrum, complete with racket-hurling and screamed obscenities and sometimes tears. This happened less and less as I got older and opponents got more mature, and by the time I was in college only genuine head-cases could be counted on to get so mad that they'd basically make themselves lose to an inferior player (viz. me). It's something of a shock, then, to watch Joyce do to his third-round Qualies opponent what I used to do to twelve-year-old rich kids, which is essentially to retrieve and avoid errors and wait for this opponent to have a temper tantrum. Because Sunday was a rainout, Joyce's third round is played Monday at 10:00 A.M., at the same time that some of the main draw's first rounds are beginning. Joyce's opponent is a guy named Mark Knowles, twenty-five, the 1986 U.S. Junior Indoor Champion, a native of the Bahamas, now known primarily as a doubles player but still a serious opponent, ranked in the world's top 200, somebody on Joyce's plateau.

Knowles is tall and thin, muscular in the corded way tall thin people are muscular, and has an amazing tan and tight blond curls and from a distance is an impressive-looking guy, though up close he has a kind of squished, buggy face and the slightly bulging eyes of a player who, I can tell, is spring-loaded on a tantrum. There's a chance to see Knowles up close because he and Joyce play their match on one of the minor courts, where spectators stand and lean over a low fence only a few yards from the court. I and Joyce's coach and Knowles's coach and beautiful girlfriend are

I still play—not competitively, but seriously—and I should confess that deep down somewhere inside I still consider myself an
extremely good tennis player, real hard to beat. Before coming to
Montreal, I'd seen professional tennis only on television, which as
has been noted does not give the viewer a very accurate picture of
how good pros are. I thus further confess that I arrived in Montreal
with some dim unconscious expectation that these professionals—

---

the only people really seriously standing and watching, though a lot of spectators
on their way to more high-profile matches pass by and stop and watch a few points
before moving on. The constant movement of civilians past the court aggrieves
Knowles no end, and sometimes he shouts caustic things to people who've started
walking away while a point is still in progress.

"Don't worry about it!" is one thing Knowles shouted at someone who moved.
"We're only playing for money! We're only professionals! Don't give it a second
thought!" Joyce, preparing to serve, will stare affectlessly straight ahead while he
waits for Knowles to finish yelling, his expression sort of like the one Vegas dealers
have when a gambler they're cleaning out is rude or abusive, a patient and unjudging look whose expression is informed by the fact that they're extremely well com-
pensated for being patient and unjudging.

Sam Aparicio describes Knowles as "brilliant but kind of erratic," and I think the
coach is being kind, because Knowles seems to me to belong on a Locked Ward
for people with serious emotional and personality disorders. He rants and throws
rackets and screams scatological curses I haven't heard since junior high. If one
of his shots hits the top of the net-cord and bounces back, Knowles will scream
"I must be the luckiest guy in the world!", his eyes protruding and mouth twisted.
For me he's an eerie echo of all the rich and well-instructed Midwest kids I used
to play and beat because they'd be unable to eat the frustration when things didn't
go their way. He seems not to notice that Joyce gets as many bad breaks and weird
bounces as he, or that passing spectators are equally distracting to both players.
Knowles seems to be one of these people who view the world's inconveniences as
specific and personal, and it makes my stomach hurt to watch him. When he hits
a ball against the fence so hard it seems to damage the ball, the umpire gives him
a warning, but in the sort of gentle compassionate voice of a kindergarten teacher to
a kid who's known to have A.D.D. I have a hard time believing that someone this
off-the-wall could rise to a serious pro plateau, though it's true that when Knowles
isn't letting his attention get scattered he's a gorgeous player, with fluid strokes and
marvelous control over spin and pace. His read on Joyce is that Joyce is a slugger
(which is true), and his tactic is to try to junk him up—change pace, vary spins, hit
drop shots to draw Joyce in, deny Joyce pace or rhythm—and because he's Joyce's
equal in firepower the tactic is sound. Joyce wins the first set in a tiebreaker. But
three times in the tiebreaker Knowles yells at migratory spectators "Don't worry! It's
only a tiebreaker in a professional match!" and is basically a wreck by the time the
first set is over, and the second set is perfunctory, a formality that Joyce concludes
as fast as possible and hurries back to the Players' Tent to pack carbohydrates and
find out whether he has to play his first round in the main draw later this same day.

at least the obscure ones, the nonstars—wouldn't be all *that* much better than I. I don't mean to imply that I'm insane: I was ready to concede that age, a nasty ankle injury in '91 that I haven't bothered to get surgically fixed yet, and a penchant for nicotine (and worse) meant that I wouldn't be able to compete physically with a young unhurt professional; but on TV (while eating junk and smoking) I'd seen pros whacking balls at each other that didn't look to be moving substantially faster than the balls I hit. In other words, I arrived at my first professional tournament with the pathetic deluded pride that attends ignorance. And I have watched the Qualies—not even the main draw yet, mind you, but the competition between sixty-four fairly low-ranked world-class players for the eight qualifying slots in the Canadian Open field—with a mixture of awe and sad surprise. I have been brought up sharply. I do not play and never have played the same game as these low-ranked pros.

The craven game I spent so much of my youth perfecting would not work against these guys. For one thing, pros simply do not make unforced errors—or at any rate they make them so rarely that there's no way they're going to make the four unforced errors in seven points necessary for me to win a game. For another thing, they will take any shot that doesn't have simply ferocious depth and pace on it and—given even a fractional moment to line up a shot—hit a winner off it. For yet another thing, their own shots have such ferocious depth and pace that there's no way I'd be able to hit more than a couple of them back at any one time. I could not meaningfully *exist* on the same court with these obscure, hungry players. Nor could you. And it's not just a matter of talent or practice. There's something else.

Monday commences the main draw, and the grounds are packed. Most of the Qualies' players are in planes high above some ocean somewhere by now.

Going to a major ATP tournament is like a cross between going to a major-league ball game and going to the fair. You can buy a Grounds Pass and wander from match to match, sampling the fare.

You can also buy specific expensive tickets for big-name matches in the Stadium and Grandstand. In the early rounds, these headline matches tend to feature the high seeds and household names— Agassi, Sampras, Chang—against main draw also-rans like Jacob Hlasek.[50]

Being a tennis spectator is different from being at a baseball game, though. Whether crowd-noise or -movement is any more distracting to someone getting ready to serve than it is to someone getting ready to shoot a free throw, players and tournaments act like it is, and play itself is supposed to be conducted in as close to funereal silence as possible.[51] If you've got a seat for a Stadium match, you can leave and return only during the break that happens after every odd-numbered game, when the players get to sit under red umbrellas for a second. Ushers cordon off the exits during play, and a concession-laden mass of spectators always stretches from just behind these ropes all the way down the slanted ramps into the Stadium's bowels, waiting to get back in.

Stade Jarry has the same sort of crumbling splendor that characterizes a lot of Montreal. The Stadium/Grandstand structure used to house the Expos before Montreal built Olympic Stadium, and it's grimy and old and creaks alarmingly when crowds enter or exit. The "Players' Lounge," which at most tournaments is a temperature-controlled salon with plush chairs and video games and multiple massage rooms, is at Stade Jarry just a big tent with canvas partitions around the locker room, no video games, just one TV, and no AC. The parking lots are inadequate and tufted with crabgrass, and the easements between courts and facilities on

---

50. Hlasek lost in the first round of the main draw Tuesday morning to obscure American Jonathan Stark, who then lost to Sampras in the second round on Wednesday in front of a capacity Stadium crowd.

51. This is in the Stadium and Grandstand, where the big names play, this ceremonial hush. Lesser players on the outlying courts have to live with spectators talking during points, people moving around so that whole rickety sets of bleachers rumble and clank, food service attendants crashing carts around on the paths just outside the windscreen or giggling and flirting in the food-prep tents just on the other side of several minor courts' fences.

the grounds are either dirt or some kind of blacktop that's decayed back to the point where it's just about dirt too. The whole thing's due to be torn down after the '95 Open's over, and a new Flushing Meadows–type tennis complex is going to be built by Tennis Canada[52] and a whole bunch of the corporations whose names are on the Stadium's brothelish bunting.

The tournament site's surrounding Parc du Jarry, on the other hand, is exquisite. From the top row of the Stadium's seats you can look out in the sunshine and see rolling grass, a public pool, a pond replete with stately fowl. In the distance to the north is the verdigrised dome of a really big church; to the west is the EKG skyline of downtown Montreal.

But so you can wander between matches, stand around watching the practice courts, join the lines for the restrooms, or elbow-fight with little kids and autograph hunters outside the Players' Tent. Or you can buy concessions. There's a booth outside one entrance to the Stadium Court that sells only Evian water. There's Spanish peanuts and fudge you can buy by the gram and eat or buy by the kilo and take home.[53] The whole Stade Jarry grounds have a standard summer-touristic reek of fried foods—French fries in cups, nachos, and in paper trays small spiraled fried things I decline to examine closely. There are two booths for Richard D's Bars, a kind of Québecois cognate for Dove Bars (and not quite as good, but pretty good). There are only two men's rooms open to the public,[54]

52. This is Canada's version of the U.S.T.A., and its logo—which obtrudes into your visual field as often as is possible here at the du Maurier Omnium—consists of the good old Canadian maple leaf with a tennis racket for a stem. It's stuff like Tennis Canada's logo you want to point to when Canadians protest that they don't understand why Americans make fun of them.

53. (though best of luck getting fudge home in this heat . . .)

54. "Le Média" has its own facilities, though they're up in the Press Box, about five flights of rickety and crowded stairs up through the Stadium's interior and then exterior and then interior, with the last flight being that dense striated iron of like a fire escape and very steep and frankly dangerous, so that when one has to "aller au pissoir" it's always a hard decision between the massed horror of the public restrooms and the Sisyphean horror of the Press bathroom, and I learn by the second day to go very easy on the Evian water and coffee as I'm wandering around.

and the lines for both always resemble a run on a midsize branch bank. There's the Rado® Smash Booth, where for $3.00 Canadian you can step inside a large cage with a much-handled racket and hit a serve into a frayed-looking net and have the speed of your serve appear on a big liquid-crystal display above the cage. Most of the people availing themselves of the Rado® Smash Booth are men, whose girlfriends watch dutifully as the men step inside the cage with the same testosteronic facial expression of men at fairs testing their marksmanship or sledge-swinging prowess—and the American men tend to be very pleased and excited at the displayed speed of their serve until it dawns on them that the readout's in kph instead of mph. There are hot dogs and hamburgers and the ambient sizzle-sound of same over near the Grandstand entrances. Just east of the Grandstand and the second men's room, there's a whole sort of cafeteria in a big tent with patio tables arrayed on Astroturf that's laid over a low deck of extremely flimsy boards so that your table trembles and your Evian bottle falls over every time somebody walks by. Starting on Monday there are a lot of Canadian girls in really short tight shorts and a lot of muscle-shirted Canadian boyfriends who scowl at you if you react to the girlfriends in the way the girlfriends' tight shorts seem designed to make anyone with a healthy endocrine system react.

There are old people who sit on red Stade Jarry park benches all day without moving.

At just about every gate and important door on the Stade Jarry grounds there are attendants, young Quebeckers paid by the tournament—whether their function is security or what remains somewhat unclear—who sit all day with walkie-talkies and red and black du Maurier visors and the catatonically bored expressions of attendants everywhere.

There are four separate booths that sell good old U.S. soft drinks, you'll be glad to know, although the booths' promo-signs for "Soft Drinks" translate literally into "Gaseous Beverages," which might explain why most Canadian Open spectators opt for Evian instead of soft drinks.

Or you can stand in front of the Canadian Open Stringer's Tent and watch the Official ATP Tour Stringer work through a small mountain of rackets, using pliers and shears and what looks like a combination blacksmith's anvil and dentist's chair. Or you can join the battalion of kids outside the Players' Tent all trying to get their Official ATP Player Trading Cards[55] autographed by players entering or exiting, and you can witness a kind of near-riot when the passing player turns out to be Sampras or Courier or Agassi, and you can even get stiff-armed by a bodyguard in wraparound shades when Brooke Shields passes too close in her own wraparounds and floppy hat.

If the mood for more serious consumption strikes, you can walk due east of the Stadium complex to the Promenade du Sportif, a kind of canvas strip mall selling every product even remotely associated with the Canadian Open: Prince, Wilson, Nike, Head, Boost® Vitamin/Energy Drink (free samples available), Swatch, Nature Valley Granola Bars,[56] Sony, and DecoTurf Inc.

And at this tournament you can (U.S. readers may want to sit down for this part) actually *buy* du Maurier–brand cigarettes—by the carton or broad flat Europack—from a special red and black booth right outside the main entrance to the Stadium Court.[57] People in Quebec smoke—heavily—and this booth does serious business. No part of Stade Jarry is nonsmoking, and at matches so many spectators are chain-smoking du Maurier cigarettes that at times a slight breeze will carry the crowd's exhaled cloud of smoke out over the court, transforming the players into nacreous silhouettes for a moment before the cloud ascends. And, in truth, accredited media

55. (a recent and rather ingenious marketing move by the ATP—I buy several just for the names)

56. It's not at all clear what N.V.G.B.'s have to do with the Omnium, and no free samples are available.

57. Du Maurier cigarettes are like Australian Sterlings or French Gauloises—full-bodied, pungent, crackly when inhaled, sweet and yeasty when exhaled, and so strong that you can feel your scalp seem to leave your skull for a moment and ride the cloud of smoke. Du Maurier–intoxication may be one reason why the Canadian Open crowds seem so generally cheery and expansive and well-behaved.

don't even have to *buy* the du Mauriers; Press Box employees will give packs out free to journalists, though they don't announce this or make a big big deal of it.

It's the little things like public smoking that remind you that Canada's not home. Or e.g. Francophone ads, and these ads' lack of even a pretense of coy subtlety—someplace between the Radisson des Gouverneurs and Stade Jarry is a huge billboard for some kind of Québecois ice cream. It's a huge photo of an ice cream cone poised at a phallic 45°, jutting, the dome of ice cream unabashedly glansular, and underneath is the pitch: "Donne-moi ta bouche."[58] The brand's own trademark slogan, at the bottom, is that it's "La glace du lait plus lechée." One of the nice things Michael Joyce and his coach do is usually let me ride with them in their courtesy car[59] between the hotel and Jarry, to sort of lurk and soak up atmosphere, etc. We pass this billboard several times a day. Finally one time I point up at the glistening phallic ad and ask Joyce whether the ad strikes him as a little heavy, overt, uncoy. Joyce looks up at the billboard—maybe for the first time, because in the car he's usually staring commuterishly straight ahead, either gathering himself into a prematch focus or exiting gradually from same—and turns to me and says in all earnestness that he's tried this particular brand of Canadian ice cream and it's not all that good.

Plus, of course, once the main draw starts, you get to look up close and live at name tennis players you're used to seeing only as arrays of pixels. One of the highlights of Tuesday's second round of the main draw is getting to watch Agassi play MaliVai Washington.

58. (= "Give me your mouth"—not subtle at all)

59. These are usually luxury cars provided by some local distributorship in return for promotional consideration. The Canadian Open's courtesy cars are BMWs, all so new they smell like glove compartments and so expensive and high-tech that their dashboards look like the control panels of nuclear reactors. The people driving the courtesy cars are usually local civilians who take a week off from work and drive a numbingly dull route back and forth between hotel and courts—their compensation consists of free tickets to certain Stadium matches and a chance to rub elbows with professional tennis players, or at least with their luggage.

Washington, the most successful black American on the Tour since Ashe, is unseeded at the Canadian Open but has been ranked as high as #11 in the world, and is dangerous, and since I loathe Agassi with a passion it's an exciting match. Agassi looks scrawny and faggy and, with his shaved skull and beretish hat and black shoes and socks and patchy goatee, like somebody just released from reform school (a look you can tell he's carefully decided on with the help of various paid image-consultants, and now cultivates). Washington, who's in dark-green shorts and a red shirt with dark-green sleeves, was a couple of years ago voted by *People* one of the 50 Prettiest Human Beings or something, and on TV is indeed real pretty but in person is awesome. From twenty yards away he looks less like a human being than like a Michelangelo anatomy sketch: his upper body the V of serious weight lifting, his leg-muscles standing out even in repose, his biceps little cannonballs of fierce-looking veins. He's beautiful but doomed, because the slowness of the Stadium Court makes it impractical for anybody except a world-class net man to rush the net against Agassi, and Washington is not a net man but a power-baseliner. He stays back and trades groundstrokes with Agassi, and even though the first set goes to a tiebreaker you can tell it's a mismatch. Agassi has less mass and flat-out speed than Washington, but he has vision and timing that give his groundstrokes way more pace. He can stay back and hit nuclear groundstrokes and force Washington until Washington eventually makes a fatal error. There are two ways to make a fatal error against Agassi: the first is the standard way, hitting it out or into the net or something; the second is to hit anything shorter than a couple feet inside the baseline, because anything that Agassi can move up on he can hit for a winner. Agassi's facial expression is the slightly smug self-aware one of somebody who's used to being looked at and automatically assumes the minute he shows up anywhere that everybody's looking at him. He's incredible to see play in person, but his domination of Washington doesn't make me like him any better; it's more like it chills me, as if I'm watching the devil play.

Television tends to level everybody out and make them seem

kind of blandly handsome, but at Montreal it turns out that a lot of the pros and stars are interesting- or even downright funny-looking. Jim Courier, former #1 but now waning and seeded tenth here,[60] looks like Howdy Doody in a hat on TV, but here he turns out to be a very big boy—the "Guide Média" lists him at 175 pounds but he's way more than that, with large smooth muscles and the gait and expression of a Mafia enforcer. Michael Chang, twenty-three and #5 in the world, sort of looks like two different people stitched crudely together: a normal upper body perched atop hugely muscular and totally hairless legs. He has a mushroom-shaped head, ink-black hair, and an expression of deep and intractable unhappiness, as unhappy a face as I've ever seen outside a Graduate Writing Program.[61] P. Sampras, in person, is mostly teeth and eyebrows, and he's got unbelievably hairy legs and forearms, hair in the sort of abundance that allows me confidently to bet that he has hair on his back and is thus at least not 100% blessed and graced by the universe. Goran Ivanisevic is large and tan and surprisingly good-looking—at least for a Croat; I always imagine Croats looking ravaged and katexic and like somebody out of a Munch lithograph—except for an incongruous and wholly absurd bowl haircut that makes him look like somebody in a Beatles tribute band. It is Ivanisevic who will beat Joyce in three sets in the main draw's

---

60. He will lose badly to Michael Stich in the round of 16, the same Stich whom Michael Joyce beat at the Lipton Championships in Key Biscayne four months before; and in fact Joyce will himself beat Courier in straight sets next week at the Infiniti Open in Los Angeles, in front of Joyce's family and friends, for one of the biggest wins of his career so far.

61. Chang's mother is here—one of the most infamous of the dreaded Tennis Parents of the men's and women's Tours, a woman who's reliably rumored to have done things like reach down her child's tennis shorts in public to check his underwear—and her attendance (she's seated hierophantically in the player-guest boxes courtside) may have something to do with the staggering woe of Chang's mien and play. Thomas Enqvist ends up beating him soundly in the quarterfinals on Wednesday night. (Enqvist, by the way, looks eerily like a young Richard Chamberlain, the Richard Chamberlain of *The Towering Inferno*, say, with this narrow, sort of rodentially patrician quality. The best thing about Enqvist is his girlfriend, who wears glasses and when she applauds a good point sort of hops up and down in her seat with refreshing uncoolness.)

second round. Czech former top-ten Petr Korda is another clastic-looking mismatch: at 6'3" and 160, he has the body of an upright greyhound and the face of—eerily, *uncannily*—a fresh-hatched chicken (plus soulless eyes that reflect no light and seem to "see" only in the way that fish's and birds' eyes "see").

And Wilander is here—Mats Wilander, Borg's heir, top-ten at age eighteen, #1 at twenty-four, now thirty and unranked and trying a comeback after years off the Tour, here cast in the role of the wily old mariner, winning on smarts. Tuesday's best big-name match is between Wilander and Stefan Edberg,[62] twenty-eight and Wilander's own heir[63] and now married to Annette Olson, Wilander's S.O. during his own glory days, which adds a delicious personal cast to the match, which Wilander wins 6–4 in the third. Wilander ends up getting all the way to the semifinals before Agassi beats him as badly as I have ever seen one professional beat another professional, the score being 6–0 6–2 and the match not nearly as close as the score would indicate.

Even more illuminating than watching pro tennis live is watching it with Sam Aparicio, Joyce's coach, who knows as much about tennis as anybody I've talked to and isn't obnoxious about it. Sam watches a lot of pro matches, scouting stuff for Michael. Watching tennis with him is like watching a movie with somebody who knows a lot about the technical aspects of film: he helps you see things you can't see alone. It turns out, for example, that there are whole geometric sublevels of strategy in a power-baseline game, all dictated by various P.B.ers' strengths and weaknesses. A P.B.er

---

62. Who himself has the blond bland good looks of a professional golfer, and is reputed to be the single dullest man on the ATP Tour and possibly in the whole world, a man whose hobby is purported to be "staring at walls" and whose quietness is not the quietness of restraint but of blankness, the verbal equivalent of a dead channel.

63. (Just as Enqvist now appears to be Edberg's heir . . . Swedish tennis tends to be like monarchic succession: they tend to have only one really great player at a time, and this player is always male, and he almost always ends up #1 in the world for a while. This is one reason marketers and endorsement-consultants are circling Enqvist like makos all through the summer.)

depends on being able to hit winners from the baseline. But, as Sam teaches me to see, Michael Chang can usually hit winners only at an acute angle, from either corner. An "inside-out" player like Jim Courier, on the other hand, can hit winners only at obtuse angles, from the center out. Hence canny and well-coached players tend to play Chang "down the middle" and Courier "out wide." One of the things that makes Agassi so good is that he's capable of hitting winners from anywhere on the court—he has no geometric restriction. Joyce, too, according to Sam, can hit a winner at any angle. He just doesn't do it quite as well as Agassi, or as often.

Michael Joyce in close-up person, like eating supper or riding in a courtesy car, looks slighter and younger than he does on-court. From close up he looks his age, which to me is basically a fetus. He's about 5'9" and 160; he's muscular but quietly so, without much definition. He likes to wear old T-shirts and a backwards cap. His hairline is receding in a subtle young-man way that makes his forehead look a little high. I forget whether he wore an earring. Michael Joyce's interests outside tennis consist mostly of big-budget movies and genre novels of the commercial paperback sort that one reads on planes. In other words, he really has no interests outside tennis. He has a tight and long-standing group of friends back home in LA, but one senses that most of his personal connections have been made via tennis. He's dated some. It's impossible to tell whether he's a virgin. It seems staggering and impossible, but my sense is he might be. Then again, I tended to idealize and distort him, I know, because of how I felt about what he could do on the court. His most revealing sexual comment is made in the context of explaining the odd type of confidence that keeps him from freezing up in a match in front of large crowds or choking on a point when there's lots of money at stake.[64] Joyce, who usually needs to pause about five beats

---

64. Nerves and choking are a huge issue in a precision-and-timing sport like tennis, and a "bad head" washes more juniors out of the competitive life than any sort of deficit in talent or drive.

to think before he answers a question, thinks the confidence is partly a matter of temperament and partly a function of hard work:

"If I'm in like a bar, and there's a really good-looking girl, I might be kind of nervous. But if there's like a thousand gorgeous girls in the stands when I'm playing, it's a different story. I'm not nervous then, when I play, because I know what I'm doing. I know what to do out there." Maybe it's good to let these be his last quoted words.

Whether or not he ends up in the top ten and a name anybody will know, Michael Joyce will remain a figure of enduring and paradoxical fascination for me. The restrictions on his life have been, in my opinion, grotesque; and in certain ways Joyce himself is a grotesque. But the radical compression of his attention and self has allowed him to become a transcendent practitioner of an art—something few of us get to be. It's allowed him to visit and test parts of his psyche that most of us do not even know for sure we have, to manifest in concrete form virtues like courage, persistence in the face of pain or exhaustion, performance under wilting scrutiny and pressure.

Michael Joyce is, in other words, a complete man (though in a grotesquely limited way). But he wants more. Not more completeness; he doesn't think in terms of virtues or transcendence. He wants to be the best, to have his name known, to hold professional trophies over his head as he patiently turns in all four directions for the media. He is an American and he wants to win. He wants this, and he will pay to have it—will pay just to pursue it, let it define him—and will pay with the regretless cheer of a man for whom issues of choice became irrelevant long ago. Already, for Joyce, at twenty-two, it's too late for anything else: he's invested too much, is in too deep. I think he's both lucky and un-. He will say he is happy and mean it. Wish him well.

1996

Democracy and Commerce at the U.S. Open

RIGHT NOW IT'S 1530H. on 3 September, the Sunday of Labor Day Weekend, the holiday that's come to represent the American summer's right bracket. But L.D.W. always falls in the middle of the U.S. Open;[1] it's the time of the third and fourth rounds, the tournament's meat, the time of trench warfare and polysyllabic names. Right now, in the National Tennis Center's special Stadium —a towering hexagon[2] whose N, S, E, and W sides have exterior banners saying "WELCOME TO THE 1995 U.S. OPEN—*A USTA EVENT*"—right now a whole inland sea of sunglasses and hats in the Stadium is rising to applaud as Pete Sampras and the Australian Mark Philippoussis are coming out on court, as scheduled, to labor. The two come out with their big bright athletic bags and their grim-looking Security escorts. The applause-acoustics are deafening. From down here near the court, looking up, the Stadium looks to be shaped like a huge wedding cake, and once past the gentler foothills of the box seats the aluminum stands seem to rise away on all sides almost vertically, so vertiginously steep that a misstep on any of the upper stairs looks like it would be certain and hideous death. The umpire sits in what looks like a lifeguard chair with little metal stirrups out front for his shoes,[3] wearing a headset-mike and

---

1. "*A USTA Event.*"

2. Actually, if you count the Grandstand Court's annex, the whole thing looks more like an ablated head w/ neck-stump.

3. There's always something extremely delicate and precarious and vulnerable-looking about the umpire's shoes projecting out over the court from a height in

Ray-Bans and holding what's either a clipboard or a laptop. The DecoTurf court is a rectangle of off-green marked out by the well-known configuration of very white lines inside a bigger rectangle of off-green; and as the players cross the whole thing E–W to their canvas chairs, photographers and cameramen converge and cluster on them like flies clustering on what flies like—the players ignore them in the way that only people who are very used to cameras can ignore cameras. The crowd is still up and applauding, a pastel mass of 20,000+. A woman in a floppy straw hat three seats over from me is talking on a cellular phone; the man next to her is trying to applaud while holding a box of popcorn and is losing a lot of popcorn over the box's starboard side. The scoreboards up over the Stadium's N and S rims are flashing pointillist-neon ads for EVIAN. Sampras, poor-postured and chestless, smiling shyly at the ground, his powder-blue shorts swimming down around his knees, looks a little like a kid wearing his father's clothes.[4] Philippoussis, who chronologically really *is* a kid, looks hulking and steroidic walking next to Sampras. Philippoussis is 6'4" and 200+ and is crossing the court with the pigeon-toed gait of a large man who's trying not to lumber, wearing the red-and-white candy-stripe Fila shirt so many of the younger Australians favor. The P.M. sun is overhead to the WSW in a sky with air so clear you can almost hear the sun combusting, and the tiny heads of the spectators way up at the top of the W bleachers are close enough to the sun's round bottom to look to be just about on fire. The players dump their long bags and begin to root through them. Their rackets are in plastic they have to unwrap. They sit in their little chairs hitting racket-faces together and cocking their heads to listen for pitch. The cameramen around

---

little metal stirrups—the blend of authority and precarious vulnerability is just one of the things that makes a tennis umpire such a compelling part of the whole show.

4. The tentish tops and near-Bermuda-length shorts of M. Jordan and the NBA have clearly infiltrated tennis. Nearly half the men in the 128 draw are wearing clothes that seem several sizes too big, and on players as fundamentally skinny and woebegone-looking as Sampras the effect is more waifish than stylish—though I have to say that weirdly oversized clothes aren't near the visual disaster that Agassi's new clunky black sneakers (also imported from basketball fashion) are.

them disperse at the umpire's command, some trailing snakes of cord. Ballboys take crumpled bits of racket plastic from under the players' chairs.

A lady making her way in that sideways-processional way past seats in the row right beneath me wears a shirt advising all onlookers that they ought to Play Hard because Life Is Short. The man on her arm wears a (too-large) designer T-shirt decorated with images of U.S. currency. A firm/pleasant usher stops them halfway across the row to check their tickets. Fifteen hundred citizens of the borough of Queens are employed at the Open today. Weekend labor. The ushers are at their fat chains stretched across the Stadium tunnels, all wearing chinos and button-down shirts. The Security guys (all large and male, not a neck or a smile in sight) wear lemon-yellow knit shirts that do not flatter their guts. Chewing-gum seems to be part of Security's issued equipment. The ballboys[5] are in blue-and-white Fila, while the line judges and umpires are in (Fila) shirts of vertical red-black stripes that make them look like very hip major-sport refs. The Stadium's capacity is supposedly 20,000 and there are at least 23,000 people here, mostly to see Pete. If there were rafters people would be hanging from them, and I will be shocked if there isn't some major screaming fall-down-the-steps- or topple-backward-over-the-rim-of-the-wall-type disaster before the match is done. The crowd down here near the court is for the most part adult-looking, businessish—in the Box Seats and pricey lower stands are neckties, sockless loafers, natty slacks, sweaters w/ arms tied across chests, straw boaters, L.L.Bean fishing hats, white caps with corporate names, jeweled bandeaux, high heels, and resplendent feminine sunhats—with a certain very gradual casualizing as the fashion-eye travels up (and up) past the progressively cheaper seats, until the vertiginous top sections of the bleachers feature an NYC sporting event's more typical fishnet shirts and beer hats and coolers and makeshift spittoons, halter tops and fluorescent

---

5. (looking more like ball-*grad students*, here, actually—several have earrings and leg hair, and one on the south side's got a big ginger beard)

nail polish and rubber thongs, w/ attendant coarse NYC-crowd noises sometimes drifting down from way up high overhead.[6] But apparently over 50% of tickets for this year's Open were pre-sold to corporations, who like to use them for the cultivation of clients and the entertainment of their own executives, and there is indeed about the Stadium crowd down here something indefinable that strongly suggests Connecticut license plates and very green lawns. In sum, the socioeconomic aura here for the day's headline match is one of management rather than labor.

The players' umbrellas and chairs and big EVIAN-labeled barrels of drinks are on either side of the umpire's chair at the base of the Stadium's western cliff face, in a long thin patch of shade that ripples when the heads of the people way overhead move, and it's cool in that shade—it's cool for me, as well, in the shade of the very large man next to me, who's wearing a gorgeous blue cord three-piecer and what seems to be a kind of huge sombrero—but the sunlight is summery, the sun (as mentioned) explosive, seeming to swell as it lowers, at 1535h. positioned about 40° above the Stadium's W battlements; and the Grandstand Court, attached to the Stadium's E flank, is knife-sliced by the well-known P.M. Grandstand shadow that Jim Courier is even now using to vivisect Kenneth Carlsen in full view of diners at Racquets (the impossible-to-get-into glass restaurant built into the wall that separates the Grandstand's W flank from the Stadium's E) and the 6,000+ crowd in there, a lot of whose nationalistic whistles and applause intrude into the Stadium's sonic fold and lend a kind of surreally incongruous soundtrack to Sampras and Philippoussis's exchanges as they warm up. Sampras is hitting with the casual economy that all the really top pros seem to warm up with, the serene nonchalance of a creature at the

6. The Open's crowds, I know, are legendary for being loud and vulgar and generally psycho, but I've got to say that most of the audiences for most of L.D.W.'s matches seem like people you'd be proud to take home and introduce to the folks. The odd bit of audible nastiness does sometimes issue from way up top in the Stadium's bleachers, but then usually only when there's been some missed call or flagrant injustice.

very top of the food chain. The Wimbledon champion's presence aside, this third-rounder has particular romance about it because it features two Greeks neither of whom are in fact from Greece, a kind of postmodern Peloponnesian War. Philippoussis, just eighteen, Patrick Rafter's doubles partner, ranked in the top 100 in this his first year on tour, potential superstar and actual heartthrob,[7] resembles Sampras, somewhat—same one-handed backhand and slight loop on the forehand's backswing, same café-au-lait coloring and Groucho eyebrows and very black hair that get glossy with sweat—but the Australian is slower afoot, and in contrast to Sampras's weird boneless grace he looks almost awkward, perilously large, his shoulders square the way heavy guys with bad backs' shoulders are square. Plus he seems to have aggression-issues that need resolving: he's hitting the ball as hard as he can even in warm-up. He seems brutish, Philippoussis does, Spartan, a big slow mechanical power-baseliner[8] with chilly malice in his eyes; and against him, Sampras, who is not exactly a moonballer, seems almost frail, cerebral, a poet, both wise and sad, tired the way only democracies get tired, his expression freighted with the same odd post-Wimbledon melancholy that's dogged him all summer through Montreal, Cincinnati, etc. Thomas Enqvist's epic 2–6 6–2 4–6 6–3 7–6 (7–5) first-rounder against Marcelo Ríos and Agassi's second-round squeaker against Corretja notwithstanding, it's tempting to see this upcoming match as the climax of the Open so far: two ethnically agnate and archetypally distinct foes, an opposition not just of styles of play but of fundamental orientations

7. Females in the crowds of this year's Australian Open apparently screamed and fainted and made with Beatlemania-like histrionics whenever Rafter or Philippoussis appeared, and it's true that on the court they are both extremely handsome guys; but it's also true that Mark Philippoussis, close up, looks amazingly like Gaby Sabatini—I mean *amazingly*, right down to the walk and the jaw line and the existentially affronted facial expression.

8. The Open's slow DecoTurf, which various rumors allege has had some kind of extra abrasive mixed in to make it even slower for the Open, favors the power-baseline game of Agassi, Courier, et al.—even netophiles like Edberg and Krajicek have been staying back and whaling through the first two rounds.

toward life, imagination, the uses of power . . . plus of course economic interests.

Covering the four walls down around the Stadium Court is a kind of tarp, chlorine-blue,[9] and on it, surrounding the court, are the white proper nouns FUJIFILM, *REDBOOK* MAGAZINE, MassMutual, U.S. OPEN '95—*A USTA EVENT*, CAFÉ de COLOMBIA (complete w/ a dotted white outline of Juan Valdez and devoted burro), INFINITI, TAMPAX, and so on.[10] Professional tennis always gets called an international sport, but it would be more accurate to call it a *multinational* sport: fiscally speaking, it exists largely as a marketing subdivision of very large corporations, and not merely of the huge Tour-underwriting conglomerates like IBM and Virginia Slims. The hard core of most professional players' earnings comes from product endorsement. Absolutely every venue and piece of equipment associated with pro events has some kind of ad on it. Even the official names of most pro tournaments are those of companies that have bid to be a "title

---

9. The Open's administration is smart about providing the right visual backdrop for world-class play. The Stadium Court at the du Maurier Ltd. in Montreal this July had yellow bleachers at the north end that, according to players, made it tough to track balls coming from that end, whereas the N.T.C's Stadium's got blue tarps and white chairs and gray chairs, and even the bleachers are high-contrast red—there's nothing even close to the YG part of the spectrum unless you count the pale-yellow shirts of the Security guys who stand courtside with the crossed arms and beady eyes of Secret Servicemen. (I've got to think the whole Seles thing is behind the high-profile Security here.)

10. The tarp ads around pro tennis courts function like ads on subways, I think. Ads on subways exploit the fact that subway rides present both a lot of mental downtime and a problem with what to look at—the windows are mostly dark, and looking directly at other people on the subway is an action that the lookee can interpret in a number of ways, some of which are uncomfortable or even hazardous—and the ads up over the windows are someplace neutral and adverting to rest the eye, and so they usually get a lot of attention. And tennis is also full of downtime—periods between points, changeovers between odd games—where the eye needs diverting. Plus, during play, the tarp acts as the immediate visual background to the players, and the eyes and cameras always follow the players—including TV—so that having your company's name hovering behind Sampras as the camera tracks him is a way both to get serious visual exposure for your company and to have that name associated, even on a subliminal level, with Sampras and tennis and excellence in general, etc. It all seems tremendously sophisticated and shrewd, psychologically speaking.

sponsor": the Canadian Open this year was the "du Maurier Ltd.
Open" (for a Canadian cigarette company), Munich was the "BMW
Open," New Haven was the "Volvo International" (next year it's to
be the "Pilot Pen International"), Cincinnati the "Thriftway ATP
Championship," and so on. The U.S. Open,[11] being a Slam and a
national championship, doesn't have a title sponsor like Munich or
Montreal; but instead of decommercializing the event, the tournament's Slam-status just makes the number of different commercial
subsidizations more dizzying. The Open has an official sponsor not
just for the tournament but for each of the tournament's various
individual *events:* Infiniti sponsors the Men's Singles, *Redbook* the
Women's Singles, MassMutual the Junior Boys, and so on.[12]

11. See FN#1 again—the strong sense I got was that you are never to say "The U.S.
Open" in any kind of public way without also saying "*A USTA Event.*" Let's let the
U.S.T.A.'s promotional appendix be implicit from now on; I don't feel like saying it
over and over. The United States Tennis Association gets something like 75% of its
yearly operating revenues from the U.S. Open, and it's probably understandable
that it would want to attach its name like a remora to the tournament's flank, but
the constant imposition of "*A USTA Event*" all over the place got a little tiresome, I
found, overtaxing the way relentless self-promotion is overtaxing, and I have to say
I got a kind of unkind thrill out by the Main Gate's turnstiles when so many people
coming in for the evening session of matches pointed up at the big sign over the
Main Gate and asked each other what the hell "USTA" was, making it rhyme with
a Boston pronunciation of "buster" or "Custer."

12. The names of all the various sponsors are on a big (*very* big) blue board just
inside the National Tennis Center's Main Gate, with the bigger events' "presenting
sponsors" on the left in huge caps, and in smaller caps on the right the names of
pres. spons. of smaller events—Men's 35s Doubles, Mixed Doubles Masters—as
well as other sponsors whose role is unclear beyond having paid a fee to sell concessions where appropriate and/or to have a PR booth on the grounds and a venue
to call their own inside the Corporate Hospitality Areas (plus of course having their
name on the v.b. blue board). Here's the whole sign's program, much reduced in
scale: in the middle (natch), "1995 U.S. OPEN—*A USTA Event*"; on the left: Infiniti,
Redbook, Prudential Securities, Chase Manhattan, Fujifilm, MassMutual; on the
right: American Express, AT&T, Ben Franklin Crafts, Café de Colombia, Canon,
Citizen Watch Company (Citizen also has its name on all the big real-time and
match-duration clocks on the Show Courts), Evian Natural Spring Water, Fila
U.S.A., The Häagen-Dazs Co. Inc., Heineken, IBM, K-Swiss, *The New York Times*
(which one kind of wonders, then, how objectively or aggressively the paper could
report the facts if like the tournament this year were really boring or poorly man-
aged or crooked somehow, etc.), NYNEX, Pepsi-Cola, Sony, Tampax (which, now
that Virginia Slims finally got PC'd out of sponsoring the WTA, put in a bid to
be the tour's new sponsor but was turned down, for reasons that haven't been

Now the umpire has ordered Play and Sampras is getting ready to serve, lifting the toe of his front foot on the toss's upswing in that distinctive way he has. I've never gotten to see Sampras play live before, and he's far more beautiful an athlete than he appears to be on TV. He's not particularly tall or muscley, but his serve is near-Wagnerian in its effect, and from this close up you can see that it's because Sampras has got some magic blend of flexibility and timing that lets him release his whole back and trunk into the serve—his whole *body* can snap the way normally just a wrist can snap—and that this has something to do with the hunched, coiled way he starts his service motion, lifting just the toe of his front foot and sighting over the racket like a man with a crossbow, a set of motions that looks ticcy and eccentric on TV but in person makes his whole body look like one big length of muscle, a kind of angry eel getting ready to writhe. Philippoussis, who likes between points to dance a little in place—perhaps to remind himself that he can indeed move if he needs to—awaits service without facial affect. His headband matches his candy-stripe shirt. The scoreboards' displays are now set for keeping score instead of flashing ads. Philippoussis's name eats up a large horizontal section of each board. The wall between Stadium and Grandstand (so on our E side) is topped by the press box, which runs along the wall's whole length and basically looks like the world's largest mobile home, all its windows' tinted shades now pulled against the P.M. sun. Three points have now yielded an ace, a service-return winner, and a long rally that ends when Philippoussis comes in on an approach that's not *quite* in the exact backhand corner and Sampras hits an incredibly top-heavy short angle past him into the ad service court. The fierceness of Sampras's backhand is something else that TV doesn't communicate well, his racket-head control more like that of one of those stocky clay-courters with forearms like joints of mutton, the topspin so

---

made publicly explicit but are probably amusing), Tiffany and Co., Wilson Sporting Goods, good old *Tennis* magazine (which is itself owned by The New York Times Co., so that the *Times* sneakily gets on the Board twice), and something called the VF Corporation.

heavy it distorts the ball's shape as the pass dips like a dropped thing. The malevolent but cyborgian Philippoussis hasn't betrayed anything like an actual facial expression yet. He also doesn't seem to perspire.[13] Two older guys in the row right behind me are exhorting Sampras in low tones, addressing him as "Petey," and I can't help thinking they're friends of the family or something. And propped up over the press box—so at about the height of a radio station's aerial—is the 1995 U.S. Open's own ad for itself. It's an enormous pointillist pastel print of an N.T.C. Stadium's crowd around an out-sized court, the perspective weirdly foreshortened, and then with the well-known Manhattan skyline ballooning in the immediate background in a way it decidedly does not in the real Flushing, Queens; and then above and beyond the billboard is the big zuc-chini of the Fuji Inc. blimp floating slowly against the cerulean of far and away the best summer sky I have ever seen around New York City. Not only is the '95 Open's L.D.W. air unhumid and in the eighties, the sunshine astringent and the breeze feathery and the sky the overvivid blue of a colorized film, but the sky's air is *clean*, the air smells fine and keen and sweet the way line-dried laundry smells, the result not only of a month without rain[14] but also this

13. Another sort of endearing thing about Sampras is the way he always sweats through his baby-blue shorts in an embarrassing way that suggests incontinence and lets the world see just where his athletic supporter's straps are (i.e. after a while the whole upper part of the shorts is sweated through except for a drier area that's the exact shape and size of a jock). This even TV's crude pictures can capture, and I think I like it so much because it humanizes Sampras and lets me identify with him in a way that the sheer preternatural beauty of his game does not. For me, similar humanizing foibles in transcendent players included McEnroe's irrational fits of pique, Lendl's and Navratilova's habit of every once in a while getting so nervous and choking so badly on a point that they looked almost spastic and the ball would actually hit the ground *before* it reached the net, and Connors's compulsive on-court touching and adjustment of his testes within his jock, as if he needed to know just where they were at all times.

14. According to M. Chang's limo driver, it's been, like, the longest rainless interval of the century for NYC. I don't know whether that's true or whether New Yorkers are being enjoined from watering the mums in their window boxes or whatever, but I do know that there hasn't been one rain-delay in the whole tournament so far, and the upper-management guys from both CBS and the U.S.T.A. are going around looking pleased in a way that's just short of gloating.

weekend of a freak high-pressure front that's spiraled southwest out of Nova Scotia's upper air and is blowing the oxides and odors that are NYC's deserved own out over New Jersey. The Stadium's bowl of air gets finer and keener the higher up in the stands you go, until, standing on top of somebody's smuggled Michelob cooler in the top row of bleachers[15] and peering over the wall due east past the edge of the press box, looking down over the big sign that says

WELCOME TO THE 1995 U.S. OPEN
A USTA Event

you can see them, Them, coming, an enormous serpentine mass, the crowd, still at 1615h. coming, what looks from this distance like everybody in New York City who hasn't retreated to the Hamptons for the long summer weekend. The U.S. Open is a big deal for NYC. Mayor Dinkins is gone—the Dinkins who used to reroute landing patterns at LaGuardia just for the Open—but even under Rudy Giuliani, for a fortnight a city that ordinarily couldn't give two chomps of its gum for a sport as patricianly non-contact as tennis is into the game in a very big way. Thirty-year-old arbitrageurs in non-rented tuxes at the Bowery Bar dissect various men's matches and speculate on how Seles's hiatus from the game will affect her endorsement contracts now that she's back. Croatian doormen bemoan Ivanisevic's early departure. On the subway, a set of tough chicks in leather and fluorescent hair concur that even though Graf and Seles and that Spanish what's-her-face with the

---

15. Ascending in the Stadium goes like this: past ten rows of dark-blue seats—actual plastic chairs, the Box Seats—then fifteen rows of light-blue seats, then eighteen rows of noticeably less comfortable gray molded-plastic seats, then (the steps by now so steep they feel the way staircases feel to a small child) uncountable rows of plain red bleachers, the land of backward Mets caps and tattoos and hightop sneakers w/ laces untied, the thick honk of Brooklyn accents, a great mass clicking of empty breeze-blown Liquor Bar cups on the cement of the bleachers' aisles . . . it's a climb during which the ears actually pop and the O_2 gets thin and the perspective on the court below becomes horrific, like a skyscraper's, the players looking insectile and the crowd moving and heaving in a nauseous way that makes the place's whole structure seem slightly to heave and sway.

hymen[16] in her name might rule, let's don't for a m.-fucking second count out the U.S's Zina G. 'cause this is her swan-song before the like bow-out. Or e.g. Friday, 1 September, the day after Agassi's five-set comeback against Corretja, a Lebanese driver on the Gray Line bus in from LaGuardia and a cigar-chewing old passenger he doesn't know from Adam bond over their shared assessments of Agassi's rehabilitation as a man:

"It is like he used to be brat, arrogant—you know what I am saying?"

"He grew up is what you're saying. Now he's got balls."

"Last night, this was a great game he played. This is what I am saying."

"He used to just be this hairball. Now he grew up. Now he's a *person*."[17]

But so they're coming, 40,000 yesterday and 41,000 today, ready to shell out $25–$30 for a ticket if they can even get one.[18] They come by infernal and Stygian IRT subway out to the end of the #7 line, the Shea-Willets stop. They converge on NE Queens via the Van Wyck and L.I. and Whitestone Expressways, the Interboro, the Grand Central Parkway, the Cross Bay, bringing much ready cash and whatever religious medals apply to parking spaces. City dwellers navigate by limo, cab, or bus the empty canyons of L.D.W.'s Manhattan, bound for 36th St. and the Tunnel or 59th and

---

16. (*sic*—no kidding)

17. Agassi's 1995 cybercrewcut, black sneakers, and weird new French-Resistance-fighter-style shirts have, at this year's Open, made him way more popular with male fans and only slightly less fascinatingly sexy for female fans. (Agassi's sex-symbolism's a phenomenon of deep mystery to most of the males I know, since we agree that we can all see clearly that Agassi's actually a runty, squishy-faced guy with a weird-shaped skull [which the crewcut's now made even more conspicuous] and the tiny-strided pigeon-toed walk of a schoolkid whose underwear's ridden up; and it remains completely inexplicable to us, Agassi's pull and hold on women.)

18. The National Tennis Center Box Office opens at 1000h., and people start lining up as early as 0600 hoping to get one of the day's Grounds Passes, and the various incentives and dramas in this A.M. line of street-savvy New Yorkers are a whole other story in themselves.

the Queensboro Bridge, then travel forever[19] up Northern Boulevard, bringing coolers and blankets and rackets and butt-cushions with GIANTS and JETS on them and sunscreen and souvenir hats from last year's Open, up Northern Blvd under circling air traffic until the landmarks start emerging—the squat neutron-blue ring of nearby Shea Stadium; the huge steel armillary sphere and Tinkertoy-shaped tower of the '39 World's Fairgrounds that adjoin the National Tennis Center in Flushing Meadows Corona Park;[20] or (if coming in from the SSW) the massive exoskeleton of a whole new N.T.C. Stadium Complex, incomplete and deeply eerie as seen from the Grand Central Pkwy, a huge exposed ribcage looming over fields of raw dirt and construction-site clutter and Dumpsters from the New Style Waste Disposal Co., w/ three huge canted cranes motionlessly erect against the northern horizon. No labor is under way on the new Stadium this Labor Day Weekend except for two hard-hatted and forlornly bored Security guys patrolling inside the site's fence.

The N.T.C.'s Main Gate is on the grounds' NE side, connected to the #7 train's subway stop and parking lots by a broad black-top promenade that leads from the commuter stations south past Park Rangers' offices and a couple of big open communitarian circles—the kind of open urban venues that look like they ought to have spurting fountains in the center, though these don't—with green benches and complex skateboarding and vigorous sinister underground commerce. At some point the promenade curves sharply west so that the Open's moving crowds pass within sight of rampant picnicking and soccer in F.M.C. Park (the "Meadows" part, apparently); then the walkway's final blacktop straightaway's enclosed by high fences topped with flags of all nations as you head

19. (no kidding: miles and miles on Northern through the long intestine of Queens NY, at least fifty traffic lights)

20. This is the actual name of the park that the U.S.T.A.'s National Tennis Center is in, a name almost perfect in its unconscious capture of northeast Queens's summertime essence, connoting as it does equal parts urban sewage, suburban *pastora*, and bludgeoning sun.

for the parallel lines for actual entry at the tournament's Main
Gate, the Gate's own tall fencing black iron and almost medievally
secure-looking and itself topped only by good old U.S. flags, with
the Open's/U.S.T.A.'s familiar greeting and self-assertion in bright
brave 160-point caps on a banner hanging over the turnstiles, of
which turnstiles there are six total but never more than three in
actual operation. The turnstiles are only for those who already
have tickets[21]—the East Bloc–length line for A.M. tickets at the Box
Office evaporates every day by around 1100h., when stern mega-
phones announce the day's sellout.

Besides the Stadium/Grandstand, there are three other N.T.C.
"Show Courts," i.e. courts with serious bleachers. At 1640h., Court
16 is running men's doubles with Eltingh-Haarhuis, the world's
#1 team, and its little wedge of aluminum stands isn't even full.
American tennis crowds seem decisively singles-oriented. Court
17 has Korda and Kulti against the Mad Bahamian Mark Knowles[22]
and his 1995 partner Daniel Nestor, the Canadian who's fun to
watch because he looks so much like an anorectic Mick Jagger.[23]
Court 18 has women's doubles with four players whose names I
don't recognize and exactly thirty-one people in the stands. (All
four of the females on 18 have bigger forearms than I do.) Natasha

21. Scalpers are asking and getting $125 for a Grounds Pass and (in at least one case)
twice that for an eleventh-row Stadium seat for the afternoon's matches. The last
straightaway of the walkway to the Gate has its healthy share of scalpers making
their elliptical pitches from the grassy edge, but (weirdly) there are just as many
furtive-looking parties standing at the edges asking loudly whether anyone passing
by has an extra ticket for sale, or would like perhaps to sell their own, as there are
scalpers. The scalpers and weird people asking to be scalped seem not even to
notice one another, all of them calling softly at once, and this makes the last pre-
Gate stretch of the promenade kind of surreally sad, a study in missed connection.

22. (Knowles has the same sort of perpetually aggrieved emotional style J. P.
McEnroe had, except in McEnroe the persecution complex often came off as the
high-tension neurosis of a true genius, whereas with Knowles it comes off simply
as whiny snarling churlish foul temper. All summer, following the Tour, the Mad
Bahamian has been the only ATP player I would watch and actually hope he got
beat, badly.)

23. (Nestor seems like a pretty good egg, though.)

Zvereva, looking incomplete without Gigi, is warming up against Amy Frazier in the Grandstand. In the Stadium, Philippoussis and Sampras have split the first two sets, 6 and 5. What a big match sounds like outside the Stadium is brief strut-rattling explosions of applause and whistles and then the odd flat amplification of the umpire speaking into the abrupt silence his speaking has created. Daniel Nestor's last name, while also Hellenistic, is Homerian,[24] thus allusive to a wartime way before Athens vs. Sparta. The fact that Sampras has won so many Grand Slam titles may have a lot to do with the fact that Slams' males' matches are the best of five sets. Best-of-fives require not just physical endurance but a special kind of emotional flexibility: in best-of-fives you can't play with full-bore intensity the whole time; you have to know when to kind of turn it on and when to lay back and conserve your psychic resources.[25] Philippoussis won the tie-break of a first set in which you got the impression that Sampras was sort of adjusting the idle on his game, trying to find the exact level he needed to reach to win. The suspense of the match isn't so much whether Sampras will win but how hard he'll have to play and how long it'll take him to find this out. Philippoussis hits very hard but has no imagination and even less flexibility. He's like a machine with just one gear: unless forced out of his rhythm by a wide-angle shot, he moves exclusively in forward-backward vectors. Sampras, on the other hand, seems to float like dander all over the court.[26] Philippoussis is like a great and terrible land army; Sampras is more naval, more of the drift-and-

24. (wise king of Pylos and all that)

25. In 1979 I once played two best-of-five matches in one day in a weird non-U.S.T.A. junior thing in suburban Chicago, and one match went five sets and the other four, and even though I was just seventeen I walked like a very old man for days afterward. And since emotional flexibility is almost impossible for a jr., I remember noticing that all of us who'd played 3/5's left the site looking utterly wrung-out emotionally, hollow-eyed, with the 1,000-yard stare of pogrom-survivors. I've had a special empathic compassion for male players in Slam events ever since, when I watch.

26. Sampras has a way of making it look like he hits a shot and dematerializes and then rematerializes someplace else in perfect position for the next shot. I have no theories about how he does this. Ken Rosewall is the only other male player in my

encircle school. Philippoussis is oligarchic: he has a will and seeks to impose it. Sampras is more democratic, i.e. more chaotic but also more human: his real job seems to be figuring out what his will exactly *is*. Not a lot of people remember that Athens actually lost the Peloponnesian War—it took thirty years, but Sparta finally ground them down. Nor do most people know that Athens actually *started* the whole bloody thing in the first place by picking on maritime allies of Sparta who were cutting into Athens's sea trade. Athens's clean-cut nice-guy image is a bit overdone—the whole exhausting affair was about commerce right from the beginning.

What's fun about having a U.S. Open '95 Media Pass is that you can go in and out of the Main Gate as often as you want. For paying customers there's no such luck: a sign by the turnstiles says ALL EXITS FINAL with multiple exclamation points. And the lines for entry at the three active turnstiles resemble those grim photos of trampling crowds at Third World soccer matches. Wizened little old men are paid by the tournament to stand by the turnstiles and take people's tickets—the same sort of wizened little old men you see at sporting-event turnstiles everywhere, the kind who always look like they should be wearing Shriners hats. Going through one turnstile right now at 1738h. is a very handsome bald black man in an extremely snazzy Dries Van Noten camelhair suit. Pushing hip-first through the next turnstile[27] is a woman in an electric-blue pantsuit of either silk or really good rayon. At the third active turnstile, a young foreignish-looking guy in an expensive flannel shirt w/ Ray-Bans and a cellular phone is having an argument with the turnstile's ticket-taker. The guy is claiming that he bought tickets for 3 Sept. but has mistakenly left them at home in Rye and will be *dam-ned* if he is going to be forced by a minimum-wage little wizened ticket-taker into going all the way back to Rye to get them and

---

memory who could seem to flicker in and out of existence like this. (E. Goolagong could do it, too, but not consistently.)

27. NYC being one of the most turnstile-intensive cities in the world, New Yorkers push through turnstiles with the same sort of elegantly casual élan that really top players evince when warming up.

then coming all the way back down here. He has his cellular phone in his hand, leaning over the ticket-taker: *surely*, he insists, there's some way to verify his ticket-holding status without his going and coming all the way back to produce the actual stupid cardboard rectangles themselves. The ticket-taker, in a blue suit that makes him look a bit like a train's conductor, is shaking his gnarled little head and has his arms raised in that simultaneously helpless but firm gesture of Can't Help You, Mac. The young man in flannel from Rye keeps flipping his cellular open and starting to dial it in a menacing way, as if threatening to get the ticket-taker in Dutch with shadowy figures from the Open's Olympian management heights the young man's got connections with; but the stolid little attendant's resolve stays firm, his face stony and his arms raised,[28] until crowd pressure from customers at the flannel man's rear and flank force him to withdraw the field.

The first thing you see when you come inside the Main Gate is teams of extremely attractive young people giving away free foil packets of Colombian Coffee from really big plastic barrels with outlines of Juan Valdez & devoted burro on them. The young people, none of whom are of Colombian extraction, are cheery and

---

28. This ticket-taker, who emerged as without a doubt my favorite character at the whole '95 Open, agreed to a brief interview but wanted his name withheld—the tournament apparently really does have shadowy Olympian upper-management figures whose wrath the employees fear. This ticket-taker is sixty-one, has worked the "'stiles" (as he calls them) at every U.S. Open since Ashe's stirring five-set defeats of both Graebner and Okker at Forest Hills in '68, thinks the Flushing Meadows N.T.C. inferior in every conceivable respect to good old Forest Hills, claims that the new half-built Stadium looming over the southern horizon is grotesque and pointless since its size will place the cheap seats at the very outer limits of human eyesight and a match seen from there will look like something seen from an incoming Boeing, plus that the new Stadium's been a boondoggle from the get-go and is lousy with corruption and malfeasance and general administrative rot—the guy is incredibly articulate and anecdotal and downright moving in his fierce attachment to a game he apparently has never once personally played, and he definitely in my opinion deserves a whole separate *Tennis* magazine profile next year. His stint at the Open each year is his two-week vacation from his regular job as a toll-taker at the infamous Throgs Neck Bridge between Queens and the southern Bronx, which fact may account for his flinty resolve in the face of intimidating tactics like somebody brandishing a cellular phone at him.

outgoing but don't seem to be terribly alert, because they keep giving me new free samples every time I go out and then come in again, so that my bookbag is now stuffed with them and I'm not going to have to buy coffee for months. The next thing you see is a barker on a raised dais urging you to purchase a Daily Drawsheet for $2.00[29] and a Program+Drawsheet for a bargain $8.00. Right near the barker is a gorgeous spanking-new Infiniti automobile on a complicated stand that places the car at a kind of dramatic plunging angle. It's not clear what the relation between a fine new automobile and professional tennis is supposed to be, but the visual conjunction of car and plunging angle is extremely impressive and compelling, and there's always a dense ring of spectators around the Infiniti, looking at it but not touching it.[30] Then, over the Daily Drawsheet pitchman's right shoulder and situated suspiciously close to the Advance Ticket Window, is what has to be one of the largest free-standing autotellers in the Western world, with its own shade-awning and three separate cash stations with controls of NASA-like sophistication and complexity and enormous signs that say the autoteller's provided through the generosity of CHASE and that it is equipped to disgorge cash via the NYCE, PLUS, VISA, CIRRUS, and MASTERCARD networks of auto-withdrawal. The lines for the autoteller are so long that they braid complexly into the lines for the nearest concession stands. These concession stands seem to have undergone a kind of metastasis since last year: they now are absolutely everywhere on the N.T.C. grounds. One strongly suspects that the inside story on how a concession at the U.S. Open is acquired would turn out to involve levels of intrigue and games-manship that make the tournament's on-court dramas look pal-lid, because it's clear that the really serious separation of spectator from his cash takes place at the N.T.C's concession venues, all of

---

29. The Daily Drawsheet has the distinction of being the single cheapest concession at the 1995 U.S. Open. A small and ice-intensive sodapop comes in second at $2.50.

30. Even though it's totally unguarded, people maintain the sort of respectful dis-tance from the plunging Infiniti that one associates with museums and velvet ropes.

which are doing business on the sort of scale enjoyed by coastal grocery and hardware stores during a Hurricane Warning. The free-standing little umbrella'd venues for Evian and Häagen-Dazs are small potatoes: there are entire miniature *strip malls* of refreshment stands gauntleting almost every sidewalk and walkway and easement on the grounds—even the annular ground-level tunnel of the Stadium/Grandstand—offering sodapop for $2.50–$3.50, $3.00 water, $3.00 little paper troughs of nachos or crosshatched disk-shaped French fries whose oil immediately soaks through the trough, $3.50 beer, $2.50 popcorn,[31] etc.[32]

31. (. . . this popcorn being the deep-yellow, highly salty kind that makes an accompanying beverage all but mandatory—same deal with the concessions' big hot doughy pretzels, Manhattan-street-corner-type pretzels glazed with those nuggets of salt so big that they just about have to be bitten off and chewed separately. U.S. Open pretzels are $3.00 except in the International Food Village on the Stadium's south side, a kind of compressed orgy of concession and crowded eating, where pretzel prices are slashed to $2.50 per.)

32. Take, e.g., a skinny little Häagen-Dazs bar—really skinny, a five-biter at most—which goes for a felonious $3.00, and as with most of the food-concessions here you feel gouged and outraged about the price right up until you bite in and discover it's a seriously good Häagen-Dazs bar. The fact is that when you're hungry from the sunshine and fresh air and match-watching and gushing sympathetic saliva from watching everybody else in the crowds chow down, the Häagen-Dazs bars aren't worth $3.00 but *are* worth about $2.50. Same deal with the sodapop and popcorn; same deal with the kraut-dogs on sale from steam-billowing Coney Island Refreshment stands for what seems at first glance like a completely insane and unacceptable $4.00—but then you find out they're really long and *really* good, and that the kraut is the really smelly gloppy kind that's revolting when you're not in the mood for kraut but rapturously yummy when you are in the mood for kraut. While I grumbled both times, I bought two separate kraut-dogs, and I have to admit that they hit the old spot with a force worth at least, say, $3.25.

I should also add that Colombian Coffee was FREE at all concession stands on the N.T.C. grounds over Labor Day Weekend—part of this year's wildly aggressive Juan Valdez–marketing blitz at Flushing Meadows. This seemed like a real good deal until it turned out that 90% of the time the concession stands would claim to be mysteriously "temporarily out" of Colombian Coffee, so that you ended up forking over $2.50 for an over-iced cup of Diet Coke instead, having at this point spent way too much time in the concession line to be able to leave empty-handed. It is not inconceivable that the concession stands really were out of coffee—"FREE" representing the price at which the demand curve reaches its most extreme point, as any marketer knows—but the hardened U.S. consumer in me still strongly suspected that a coffee-related Bait and Switch was in operation at some of these stands, at which the guys behind the counter managed to give the impression that they were on some kind of Rikers Island work-release program or were moonlighting from

Now a huge roar that makes the whole Stadium's superstructure wobble signifies that the forces of democracy and human freedom have won the third set.[33] It's quite clear that Sampras has found his cruising altitude and that Philippoussis is going to take the first set he won and treasure it and go home to do more bench-presses in preparation for the ATP's indoor season.

I do not know who a certain Ms. or Mr. Feron is, but s/he must be a fearsomely powerful figure in the New York sports-concession industry indeed, because a good 80% of all concession booths at the '95 Open have signs that say FERON'S on them. This goes not only for the edible concessions—whose stands have various names but all of whose workers seem to have pale-blue FERON'S shirts on—but also for the endless rows of souvenir- and tennis-related-

---

their real occupation as late-night threatening-type lurkers at Port Authority and Penn Station.

Nevertheless, the point is that every concession stand in the N.T.C. had constant long lines in front of it and that a good 66% of the crowds in the Stadium and Grandstand and at the Show Courts could be seen ingesting some sort of concession-stand item at any given time.

33. And in order to be properly impressed by the volume of concessions consumption, you need to keep in mind what a hassle it is to go get concessions when you're watching a pro match. Take the Stadium for example. You can leave your seat only during the ninety-second break between odd games, then you have to sort of slalom down crowded Stadium ramps to the nearest concession stand, hold your place in a long and Hobbesian line, hand over a gouge-scale sum, and then schlep back up the ramp, bobbing and weaving to keep people's elbows from knocking your dearly bought concessions out of your hands and adding them to the crunchy organic substratum of spilled concessions you're walking on . . . and of course by the time you find the ramp back to your section of seats the original ninety-second break in the action is long over—as, usually, is the next one after that, so you've now missed at least two games—and play is again under way, and the ushers at the fat chains prevent re-entry, and you have to stand there in an unventilated cement corridor with a sticky and acclivated floor, mashed in with a whole lot of other people who also left to get concessions and are now waiting until the next break to get back to their seats, all of you huddled there with your ice melting and kraut congealing and trying to stand on tip-toe and peer ahead to the tiny chained arch of light at the end of the tunnel and maybe catch a green glimpse of ball or some surreal fragment of Philippoussis's left thigh as he thunders in toward the net or something. . . . New Yorkers' patience w/r/t crowds and lines and gouging and waiting is extraordinarily impressive if you're not used to it; they can all stand quiescent in airless venues for extended periods, their eyes' expressions that unique NYC combination of Zen meditation and clinical depression, clearly unhappy but never complaining.

product booths that flank whatever of the grounds' Hellesponts aren't flanked by food booths already. The really hard-core, big-ticket souvenirs are sold on the Stadium's E side, in an area between the plunging Infiniti and the IBM Match-In-Progress Board. There's racketry and footwear and gear bags and warm-ups and T-shirts for sale at separate booths for Yonex, Fila, Nike,[34] Head, and William Serbin. There's a U.S.T.A. booth offering free U.S.T.A. T-shirts with a paid U.S.T.A. membership (which membership is essentially worthless unless you want to play in U.S.T.A.-sanctioned events, in which case you have no choice but to enlist). But any item with a "U.S. OPEN '95" mention on it is sold exclusively out of a FERON'S booth. Of these booths there are "0/40 at FERON'S," "FERON'S U.S. Open Silks," and "FERON'S U.S. Open Specials."[35] It's not at all clear what the term "Specials" is meant to signify in terms of price: U.S. Open '95 T-shirts are $22.00 and $25.00. Tank-tops even more. Visors $18.00 and up. Sweatshirts are $49.00 and $54.00, depending on whether they're the dusty, acid-washed autumn colors so popular this year.

It's also clear that the sea-lanes of trade between FERON'S itself and the good old United States Tennis Association are wide open, because no official FERON'S souvenir says "U.S. Open '95" without also saying *A USTA Event* right underneath.

---

34. The single most popular souvenir at the '95 Open seems to be a plain white bandanna with that little disembodied Nike trademark wing* that goes right on your forehead if you wrap the thing just right over your head. A fashion accessory made popular by you know whom. Just about every little kid I spotted at Flushing Meadows was sporting one of these white Nike bandannas, and a fairly common sight on Sunday was a harried parent trying to tie a bandanna just right to position the Nike wing over a junior forehead while his kid stood on first one foot and then the other in impatience. (You do not want to know the retail price of these bandannas, believe me.)

* The classico-Peloponnesian implications of *Nike* and of having all these kids running around with Nike wings on their foreheads like Lenten ash seem too obvious to spend much time belaboring.

35. There are at least four of these "U.S. Open Specials at FERON'S" booths at various high-traffic spots all over the N.T.C. grounds. The two distinctive things about the FERON'S clothing booths are (1) that they have separate registers for cash and Major Credit Card purchases, and (2) that none of the employees at any of these registers seems to be older than about eleven.

The grounds don't exactly empty out between the end of the after-noon's slate of matches and the start of the evening's,[36] but the crowds do thin a little. Flushing Meadows gets chilly and pretty as the twilight starts. It's about 1900h., that time when the sun hasn't gone down yet but everything seems to be in something else's shadow. The ticket-takers at the Main Gate's turnstiles change shifts, and the consumers coming down the promenade are now dressed more in jeans and sweaters than shorts and thongs. Lights over all the N.T.C. courts go on together with an enormous *thunk.* The courtlight gives the underbelly of the hanging Fuji Blimp a weird ghostly glow. There's more serious, 5-Food-Group, dinner-ish eating now going on at the International Food Village and in the Corporate Hospitality Areas. Sampras and Philippoussis have quit the field in the Stadium, Sampras bearing his shield and the Australian carried out upon his own (as it were). Arantxa Sánchez-Vicario and Mary Joe Fernandez are now warming up on the Sta-dium Court while people in the bleachers try to stagger very care-fully down the steps to get out, lugging their coolers and cushions, looking simultaneously sunburned and cold. Coming up on the Grandstand Court is a mixed-doubles match I'm looking forward to because one of the teams on the program has the marvelous name "Boogert-Oosting." Various tangential singles matches are under way on Courts 16–18, and something that's fun is to go over to these Show Courts and not to go all the way in and sit in the lit-tle sets of stands but to stand on the path outside the heavy green windscreens around the Show Courts and watch the little stripe of bare fence near the bottom for the movement of feet and to try to extrapolate from the feet's movement what's going on in each point. One unbelievably huge pair of sneakers under the screen on Court 16 turns out—sure enough—to belong to Richard Krajicek, the 6'6" Dutchman who plays like a mad crane. These shoes have to be 16EEEs at least; you wouldn't believe it. I am holding a $4.00

---

36. Tickets are sold separately for the day and evening sessions, and there are very complicated mechanisms in place to keep people with day-session tickets from lurking past 2000h. and mooching free evening spectation.

kraut-dog and sodapop I would very much like to find someplace isolated and quiet to consume.

It is not at all quiet outside the Main Gate as true evening falls. Not only does the combined em- and immigration of crowds for the different Sessions make the whole promenade from Gate to subway stop and parking lots resemble the fall of Saigon. It's especially unquiet out here *economically*. I don't know whether this magazine will run an aperçu of what all's going on out here as the sun falls, but I don't see why not, because it's not all that surprising. Since the 1995 U.S. Open is primarily—unabashedly—about commerce, and since commerce is by its nature *uncontainable*, it shouldn't be at all surprising that the most vigorous crepuscular commerce is taking place out here, outside the tournament's fence and Gate, in markets of all shade and hue. I have, e.g., in the last twenty minutes received three separate solicitations to buy pot (all wildly overpriced). The sweet burnt-pine smell of reefer is in the air all over out here, and one young guy in oversized fatigue pants is smoking a bone on a bench right next to a very neat and dapper old gentleman who's sitting with his hands folded primly and not giving any indication he smells anything untoward.[37] Scalpers have upped the pressure of their pitches in the lengthening shadows and are practically applying half nelsons to anybody on the promenade who seems even possibly to be looking for something, even if that something is just a quiet isolated place to eat a kraut-dog.[38] As mentioned *supra*, I'm

37. New Yorkers also have an amazing ability to mind their own business and attend to themselves and not notice anything untoward going on, an ability that impresses me every time I come here and that always seems to lie somewhere on the continuum between stoicism and catatonia.

38. You'll doubtless by the way be happy to know that I did, over half an hour later, find a quiet place to hunch and gnaw supper. One of the gratuitously cool things the '95 Open does is open up a few of the minor National Tennis Center courts to regular public play once the sun's gone down. This is why some of the people in the Stadium crowd had rackets, I bet. Anyway, it seems decent of them, and you can imagine what a thrill it must be for a couple of little kids to play on a court with vestigial rubber from an afternoon of pro sneakers still on it—the civilians playing clearly feel important, and they get a lot of attention from passersby on the paths

the proud possessor of a U.S. Open '95 Media Pass—which consists of a necklace of nylon cord from which hangs a large plastic card w/ a direly unflattering little photo of me that hangs against my chest at about the level of a sommelier's tasting cup—and twice this evening outside the Main Gate I've been approached by somebody wanting to borrow the Media Pass and then slip it back to me through the black fence once they've strolled inside. One offer was a straight-out bribe, but the other involved a distinguished and corporate-looking gray-haired guy in green golfer's slacks who had a complex tale of woe about a tubercular niece or something who'd paid a surprise long-distance visit to NYC and whose fondest wish was to get into the U.S. Open and that tickets were sold out, etc.[39] I observed at least one turnstile's ticket-taker (not the flinty-eyed Throgs Neck ticket-taker) receive some sort of subtle maître-d'ish payment for allowing somebody to bring in something spectators were by no stretch of the imagination allowed to bring into the

---

who are now conditioned to watch intently whenever they hear ball sounds, and it's interesting to watch the passersby's faces change after two or three seconds when they realize who and what they're watching. The little sets of bleachers for these minor public-play courts are, understandably, empty; and it was on one such little set of stands that I ate. A thirtyish guy and his wife were playing, the wife wearing a sun visor that looked a little gratuitous, the husband overhitting the way an afternoon of watching pros whale the hell out of the ball will make a man overhit. The only other person in the stands was one of the attractive young PR people who'd given me so much free coffee all day out by the M.G., sitting in her Valdez-outline T-shirt and eating something steamy out of a partitioned Styrofoam tray whose attached lid was folded back. Her professional smile and eye-twinkles were gone, so that she looked now more like the hard young New Yorker she was. As she ate she stared impassively at the husband whaling balls at his wife. She was clearly there for the same reason I was, to have some space and quiet while she ate, plus some downtime in which to rest her face from its cheery marketing expression. I felt a kind of bond between us, and from the opposite end of the bleachers where I was eating I cleared my throat and said, "Boy, it's good to find a place to be alone for a minute, isn't it?" The lady never looked around from the court as she cleared her mouth and said, "It was until a second ago."

39. (Both these solicitations had their appeal—the straight-out-bribe one especially—and only a fear of getting caught and of having to inform *Tennis* magazine that my Media Pass had been revoked because I'd been nabbed renting it out on the black market kept me from making my own stab at '95 Open free enterprise.)

N.T.C.[40] If you don't have a Stadium ticket but have the NYC savvy and financial resources, certain Stadium ushers are said (by two separate reliable sources) to be willing to place you in a vacant seat—sometimes a really up-close and desirable seat—for a sub-rosa fee, and a percentage of this fee is then apparently kicked back to a certain enterprising person or persons in the National Tennis Center who know of seats that for one reason or another aren't going to be occupied during a certain interval and relay this information to ushers (for a price). Part of the beauty of the tennis here is the way the artistry and energy are bounded by specific lines on court, but the beauty of the commerce is the way it's un- and never bounded. It's all sort of hypnotic at night. The plunging Infiniti's leather interior gets somehow mysteriously illuminated when the sun goes down, so that from a distance the car seems like a beacon. Trash-can fires appear in F.M.C. Park's distance, and the #7 train's interior's also alit as it pulls into the overground Shea stop to the north. At about 2015h. there's a fracas near the I.F. Village involving some unscrupulous/enterprising employee of whatever company actually makes the "'95 Open"–emblazoned T-shirts and hats and c. for the souvenir booths, who's apparently diverted boxes and boxes of the shirts and stuff and is going around the grounds selling them on the sly at prices way below the booths' prices,[41] and N.T.C. Security's involved, as well as—incongruously—what look like two Fire Department guys in slickers and fireman hats. It's on the whole kind of a younger and rowdier and more potentially sinister crowd that's coming in for the evening session. Their faces are stonier; eye contact seems hazardous the way eye contact on subways can be hazardous. The women tend to be dressed in ways that let you know just what they'd look like without any clothes on.

Plus food: the various extracurricular food scams haven't yet

---

40. You wouldn't believe me if I specified what it was, and it'd require a lot of space and context to make sense of, and this in an article that's already pretty clearly running over budget and straying from its original focused L.D.W. assignment.

41. (More power to him, on my view.)

been mentioned. Imagine the opportunities—not only the over-priced all-cash concession stands but the enormous tented kitch-ens for the Corporate Hospitality Areas and the "U.S. Open Club" for V.I.P.s and so on, the massive sizzle and clatter of high-volume prep from these kitchens off along the south parts of the Main Gate. Let's not even get into the little easements behind the strips of food stands, the furtive and on the whole unauthorized-looking deliveries and removals of large boxes, the various transactions and scurryings. Forget examples of that. Here's a different incident. Let's close L.D.W. with this:

Some of the time it's hard even to know what it is you're seeing take place. In one of the big communitarian fountainless circles that the promenade opens into as it leads to the Main Gate—the circle closest to the Gate, this one is—one of the circle's green benches is controlled by gypsy-cab and -limo drivers waiting for anybody exiting who needs a gypsy-type ride back to Rye or Rock-away or wherever. Half a dozen of these guys sit on this bench in their cabbies' berets, waiting around, smoking cigars, talking shit, etc. I'm on the next bench trying to organize my notes. This is at about 2100h., late. From this circle you can see the rear flaps of some of the tented high-volume kitchens. Through one of these flaps now emerges a stocky young guy in the unmistakable tall hat and whites of a kitchen worker (though on his feet are $200 Air Jordans so new they glow in the N.T.C.'s ambient light, so he looks like he's floating). The kitchen worker's carrying a broad low card-board box through the employee- and Media Pass-entrance in the Gate and down the promenade and across the circle, making for the bench with the cabbies. The cabbies are making gestures like: Finally, Thank God. One of the cabbies rises and moves out and meets the kitchen worker; something subtle occurs between their hands that indicates a transfer of funds; and now the cabbie bears the box back to the bench, where the rest of the drivers circle and grab and reveal that the box is full of supper—burgers, chicken legs, wieners, etc. Vague contented noises from the cabbies on the bench as they dig in.

"Goddamn rip-off," says a well-dressed Italian man next to me on my bench.

I say, "Pardon me?"

"Ripping the fucking place off," the well-dressed Italian man says, indicating with a hand gesture the kitchen worker, who's now making his way quickly back to the kitchen tent, hand in his pocket. The Italian man has a small filtered cigar in his mouth and a disgusted look and is sitting back with his legs crossed and his elbows up on the bench's back's top in that insouciant way savvy New Yorkers sit on park benches. He has heavy brows and wingtips and a Eurocut silk pinstripe suit of the type that Cagney-era gangsters wore. You half expect him to have a white fedora and violin case. But it turns out, when he gives me his card, that he's a legit businessman, a concessioneer, here to labor instead of recreate/consume; he's scouting out possibilities for opening a couple of stands here at next year's Open, when the new Stadium's up and running and even more vigorous attendance and commerce can be foreseen. The stands he wants to open'll sell gyros, he says. He's not Italian after all.

1996

Federer Both Flesh and Not

ALMOST ANYONE WHO LOVES tennis and follows the men's tour on television has, over the last few years, had what might be termed Federer Moments. These are times, watching the young Swiss at play, when the jaw drops and eyes protrude and sounds are made that bring spouses in from other rooms to see if you're OK. The Moments are more intense if you've played enough tennis to understand the impossibility of what you just saw him do. We've all got our examples. Here is one. It's the finals of the 2005 U.S. Open, Federer serving to Andre Agassi early in the fourth set. There's a medium-long exchange of groundstrokes, one with the distinctive butterfly shape of today's power-baseline game, Federer and Agassi yanking each other from side to side, each trying to set up the baseline winner . . . until suddenly Agassi hits a hard heavy crosscourt backhand that pulls Federer way out wide to his ad (= his left) side, and Federer gets to it but slices the stretch backhand short, a couple feet past the service line, which of course is the sort of thing Agassi dines out on, and as Federer's scrambling to reverse and get back to center, Agassi's moving in to take the short ball on the rise, and he smacks it hard right back into the same ad corner, trying to wrong-foot Federer, which in fact he does—Federer's still near the corner but running toward the centerline, and the ball's heading to a point behind him now, where he just was, and there's no time to turn his body around, and Agassi's following the shot in to the net at an angle from the backhand side . . . and what Federer now does is somehow instantly reverse thrust and sort of skip backward three or four steps, impossibly fast, to hit a forehand out of his backhand corner, all his weight moving backward, and the forehand is a topspin screamer down the line past Agassi at net, who lunges for it but the ball's past him, and it flies straight down the sideline and lands exactly in the deuce corner of Agassi's side, a winner—Federer's still dancing backward as it lands. And there's that familiar little second of shocked silence from the New York crowd before it erupts, and John McEnroe with his color man's headset on TV says (mostly to himself, it sounds like), "How do you hit a winner from that position?" And he's right: given Agassi's position and world-class quickness, Federer had to send that ball down a two-inch pipe of space in order to pass him, which he did, moving backward, with no setup time and none of his weight behind the shot. It was impossible. It was like something out of *The Matrix*. I don't know what-all sounds were involved, but my spouse says she hurried in and there was popcorn all over the couch and I was down on one knee and my eyeballs looked like novelty-shop eyeballs.

Anyway, that's one example of a Federer Moment, and that was merely on TV—and the truth is that TV tennis is to live tennis pretty much as video porn is to the felt reality of human love.

Journalistically speaking, there is no hot news to offer you about Roger Federer. He is, at twenty-five, the best tennis player currently alive. Maybe the best ever. Bios and profiles abound. *60 Minutes* did a feature on him just last year. Anything you want to know about Mr. Roger N.M.I. Federer—his background, his hometown of Basel, his parents' sane and unexploitative support of his talent, his junior tennis career, his early problems with fragility and temper, his beloved junior coach, how that coach's accidental death in 2002 both shattered and annealed Federer and helped make him what he now is, Federer's thirty-nine career singles titles, his eight Grand Slams, his unusually steady and mature commitment to the girlfriend who travels with him (which on the men's tour is rare) and handles his affairs (which on the men's tour is unheard-of), his old-school stoicism and mental toughness and good sportsmanship and evident overall decency and thoughtfulness and charitable largesse—it's all just a Google search away. Knock yourself out.

This present article is more about a spectator's experience of Federer, and its context. The specific thesis here is that if you've never seen the young man play live, and then do, in person, on the sacred grass of Wimbledon, through the literally withering heat and then wind and rain of the '06 fortnight, then you are apt to have what one of the tournament's press bus drivers describes as a "bloody near-religious experience." It may be tempting, at first, to hear a phrase like this as just one more of the overheated tropes that people resort to as they try to describe the feeling of Federer Moments. But the driver's phrase turns out to be true—literally, for an instant ecstatically—though it takes some time and serious watching to see this truth emerge.

Beauty is not the goal of competitive sports, but high-level sports are a prime venue for the expression of human beauty. The relation is roughly that of courage to war.

The human beauty we're talking about here is beauty of a particular type; it might be called kinetic beauty. Its power and appeal are universal. It has nothing to do with sex or cultural norms. What it seems to have to do with, really, is human beings' reconciliation with the fact of having a body.[1]

Of course, in men's sports no one ever talks about beauty, or grace, or the body. Men may profess their "love" of sports, but that

---

1. There's a great deal that's bad about having a body. If this is not so obviously true that no one needs examples, we can just quickly mention pain, sores, odors, nausea, aging, gravity, sepsis, clumsiness, illness, limits—every last schism between our physical wills and our actual capacities. Can anyone doubt we need help being reconciled? Crave it? It's your body that dies, after all.

There are wonderful things about having a body, too, obviously—it's just that these things are much harder to feel and appreciate in real time. Rather like certain kinds of rare, peak-type sensuous epiphanies ("I'm so glad I have eyes to see this sunrise!" etc.), great athletes seem to catalyze our awareness of how glorious it is to touch and perceive, move through space, interact with matter. Granted, what great athletes can do with their bodies are things that the rest of us can only dream of. But these dreams are important—they make up for a lot.

love must always be cast and enacted in the symbology of war: elimination vs. advance, hierarchy of rank and standing, obsessive stats and technical analysis, tribal and/or nationalist fervor, uniforms, mass noise, banners, chest-thumping, face-painting, etc. For reasons that are not well understood, war's codes are safer for most of us than love's. You too may find them so, in which case Spain's mesomorphic and totally martial Rafael Nadal is the man's man for you—he of the unsleeved biceps and Kabuki self-exhortations. Plus Nadal is also Federer's nemesis, and the big surprise of this year's Wimbledon, since he's a clay-court specialist and no one expected him to make it past the first few rounds here. Whereas Federer, through the semifinals, has provided no surprise or competitive drama at all. He's outplayed each opponent so completely that the TV and print press are worried his matches are dull and can't compete effectively with the nationalist fervor of the World Cup.[2]

July 9's men's final, though, is everyone's dream. Nadal vs. Federer is a replay of last month's French Open final, which Nadal won. Federer has so far lost only four matches all year, but they've all been to Nadal. Still, most of these matches have been on slow clay, Nadal's best surface. Grass is Federer's best. On the other hand, the first week's heat has baked out some of the Wimbledon courts' slickness and made them slower. There's also the fact that Nadal has adjusted his clay-based game to grass—moving in closer to the baseline on his groundstrokes, amping up his serve, overcoming his allergy to the net. He beat the absolute shit out of Agassi in the third round. The networks are in ecstasies. Before the match, on Centre Court, behind the glass slits above the south backstop, as the linesmen are coming out on court in their new Ralph Lauren uniforms that look so much like children's navalwear, the broadcast commentators can be seen practically bouncing up and down in

2. The U.S. media here are especially worried because no Americans of either sex survived into even the quarterfinals this year. (If you're into obscure statistics, it's the first time this has happened at Wimbledon since 1911.)

their chairs. This Wimbledon final's got the revenge narrative, the king-vs.-regicide dynamic, the stark character contrasts. It's the passionate machismo of southern Europe versus the intricate clinical artistry of the north. Dionysus and Apollo. Cleaver and scalpel. Southpaw and righty. Numbers 2 and 1 in the world. Nadal, the man who's taken the modern power-baseline game just as far as it goes . . . versus a man who's transfigured that modern game, whose precision and variety are as big a deal as his pace and foot-speed, but who may be peculiarly vulnerable to, or psyched out by, that first man. A British sportswriter, exulting with his mates in the press section, says, twice, "It's going to be a war."

Plus it's in the cathedral of Centre Court. And the men's final is always on the fortnight's second Sunday, the symbolism of which Wimbledon emphasizes by always omitting play on the first Sunday. And the spattery gale that has knocked over parking signs and everted umbrellas all morning suddenly quits an hour before match time, the sun emerging just as Centre Court's tarp is rolled back and the net posts are driven home.

Federer and Nadal come out to applause, make their ritual bows to the nobles' box. The Swiss is in the buttermilk-colored sport coat that Nike's gotten him to wear for Wimbledon this year. On Federer, and perhaps on him alone, it doesn't look absurd with shorts and sneakers. The Spaniard eschews all warm-up clothing, so you have to look at his muscles right away. He and the Swiss are both in all-Nike, up to the very same kind of tied white Nike hankie with the swoosh positioned right above the third eye. Nadal tucks his hair under his hankie, but Federer doesn't, and smoothing and fussing with the bits of hair that fall over the hankie is the main Federer tic TV viewers get to see; likewise Nadal's obsessive retreat to the ballboy's towel between points. There happen to be other tics and habits, though, tiny perks of live viewing. There's the great care Roger Federer takes to hang the sport coat over his spare courtside chair's back, just so, to keep it from wrinkling—he's done this before each match here, and something about it seems childlike and weirdly sweet. Or the way he inevitably changes out his racket sometime in the second set, the new one always in the same clear plastic bag closed with blue tape, which he takes off carefully and always hands to a ballboy to dispose of. There's Nadal's habit of constantly picking his long shorts out of his bottom as he bounces the ball before serving, his way of always cutting his eyes warily from side to side as he walks the baseline, like a convict expecting to be shanked. And something odd on the Swiss's serve, if you look very closely. Holding ball and racket out in front, just before starting the motion, Federer always places the ball precisely in the V-shaped gap of the racket's throat, just below the head, just for an instant. If the fit isn't perfect, he adjusts the ball until it is. It happens very fast, but also every time, on both first serves and second.

Nadal and Federer now warm each other up for precisely ten minutes; the umpire keeps time. There's a very definite order and etiquette to these pro warm-ups, which is something that television has decided you're not interested in seeing. Centre Court holds thirteen thousand and change. Another several thousand have done what people here do willingly every year, which is to pay a stiff General Admission at the gate and then gather, with hampers and mosquito spray, to watch the match on an enormous TV screen outside Court 1. Your guess here is probably as good as anyone's.

Right before play, up at the net, there's a ceremonial coin-toss to see who'll serve first. It's another Wimbledon ritual. The honorary coin-tosser this year is William Caines, assisted by the umpire and tournament referee. William Caines is a seven-year-old from Kent who contracted liver cancer at age two and somehow survived after surgery and horrific chemo. He's here representing Cancer Research UK. He's blond and pink-cheeked and comes up to about Federer's waist. The crowd roars its approval of the honorary toss. Federer smiles distantly the whole time. Nadal, just across the net, keeps dancing in place like a boxer, swinging his arms from side to side. I'm not sure whether the U.S. networks show the coin-toss or not, whether this ceremony's part of their contractual obligation or whether they get to cut to commercial. As William Caines is ushered off, there's more cheering, but it's scattered and disorganized;

most of the crowd can't quite tell what to do. It's like once the ritual's over, the reality of why this child was part of it sinks in. There's
a feeling of something important, something both uncomfortable
and not, about a child with cancer tossing this dream-final's coin.
The feeling, what-all it might mean, has a tip-of-the-tongue-type
quality that remains elusive for at least the first two sets.[3]

A top athlete's beauty is next to impossible to describe directly. Or
to evoke. Federer's forehand is a great liquid whip, his backhand a
one-hander that he can drive flat, load with topspin, or slice—the
slice with such snap that the ball turns shapes in the air and skids
on the grass to maybe ankle height. His serve has world-class pace
and a degree of placement and variety no one else comes close to;
the service motion is lithe and uneccentric, distinctive (on TV)

---

3. Actually, this is not the only Federer-and-sick-child incident of Wimbledon's
second week. Three days prior to the men's final, a Special One-on-One Interview
with Mr. Roger Federer* takes place in a small, crowded International Tennis Fed-
eration office just off the third floor of the Press Center. Right afterward, as the ATP
player-rep is ushering Federer out the back door for his next scheduled obligation,
one of the ITF guys (who's been talking loudly on the telephone through the whole
Special Interview) now comes up and asks for a moment of Roger's time. The man,
who has the same slight, generically foreign accent as all ITF guys, says: "Listen, I
hate doing this. I don't do this, normally. It's for my neighbor. His kid has a disease.
They will do a fund-raiser, it's planned, and I'm asking can you sign a shirt or something, you know—something." He looks mortified. The ATP rep is glaring at him.
Federer, though, just nods, shrugs: "No problem. I'll bring it tomorrow." Tomorrow's the men's semifinal. Evidently the ITF guy has meant one of Federer's own
shirts, maybe from the match, with Federer's actual sweat on it. (Federer throws his
used wristbands into the crowd after matches, and the people they land on seem
pleased rather than grossed out.) The ITF guy, after thanking Federer three times
very fast, shakes his head: "I hate doing this." Federer, still halfway out the door: "It's
no problem." And it isn't. Like all pros, Federer changes his shirt a few times during
matches, and he can just have somebody save one, and then he'll sign it. It's not like
Federer's being Gandhi here—he doesn't stop and ask for details about the kid or
his illness. He doesn't pretend to care more than he does. The request is just one
more small, mildly distracting obligation he has to deal with. But he does say yes,
and he will remember—you can tell. And it won't distract him; he won't permit it.
He's good at this kind of stuff, too.

*(Only considerations of space and basic believability prevent a full description of
the hassles involved in securing such a One-on-One. In brief, it's rather like the old
story of someone climbing an enormous mountain to talk to the man seated lotus on
top, except in this case the mountain is composed entirely of sports-bureaucrats.)

only in a certain eel-like all-body snap at the moment of impact. His anticipation and court sense are otherworldly, and his footwork is the best in the game—as a child, he was also a soccer prodigy. All this is true, and yet none of it really explains anything or evokes the experience of watching this man play. Of witnessing, firsthand, the beauty and genius of his game. You more have to come at the aesthetic stuff obliquely, to talk around it, or—as Aquinas did with his own ineffable subject—to try to define it in terms of what it is not.

One thing it is not is televisable. At least not entirely. TV tennis has its advantages, but these advantages have disadvantages, and chief among them is a certain illusion of intimacy. Television's slow-mo replays, its close-ups and graphics, all so privilege viewers that we're not even aware of how much is lost in broadcast. And a large part of what's lost is the sheer physicality of top tennis, a sense of the speeds at which the ball is moving and the players are reacting. This loss is simple to explain. TV's priority, during a point, is coverage of the whole court, a comprehensive view, so that viewers can see both players and the overall geometry of the exchange. TV therefore chooses a specular vantage that is overhead and behind one baseline. You, the viewer, are above and looking down from behind the court. This perspective, as any art student will tell you, "foreshortens" that court. Real tennis, after all, is three-dimensional, but a TV screen's image is only 2-D. The dimension that's lost (or rather distorted) on the screen is the real court's length, the seventy-eight feet between baselines; and the speed with which the ball traverses this length is a shot's pace, which on TV is obscured, and in person is fearsome to behold. That may sound abstract or overblown, in which case by all means go in person to some professional tournament—especially to the outer courts in early rounds, where you can sit twenty feet from the sideline—and sample the difference for yourself. If you've watched tennis only on television, you simply have no idea how hard these pros are hitting the ball, how fast the ball is moving,[4] how little time

4. Top men's serves often reach speeds of 125–135 mph, true, but what all the radar signs and graphics neglect to tell you is that male power-baseliners' groundstrokes

the players have to get to it, and how quickly they're able to move and rotate and strike and recover. And none are faster, or more deceptively effortless about it, than Roger Federer.

Interestingly, what is less obscured in TV coverage is Federer's intelligence, since this intelligence often manifests as angle. Federer is able to see, or create, gaps and angles for winners that no one else can envision, and television's perspective is perfect for viewing and reviewing these Federer Moments. What's harder to appreciate on TV is that these spectacular-looking angles and winners are not coming from nowhere—they're often set up several shots ahead, and depend as much on Federer's manipulation of opponents' positions as they do on the pace or placement of the coup de grâce. And understanding how and why Federer is able to move other world-class athletes around this way requires, in turn, a better technical understanding of the modern power-baseline game than TV—again—is set up to provide.

Wimbledon is strange. Verily it is the game's Mecca, the cathedral of tennis; but it would be easier to sustain the appropriate level of on-site veneration if the tournament weren't so intent on reminding you over and over that it's the cathedral of tennis. There's a peculiar mix of stodgy self-satisfaction and relentless self-promotion and -branding. It's a bit like the sort of authority figure whose office wall has every last plaque, diploma, and award he's ever gotten, and every time you come into the office you're forced to look at the wall and say something to indicate that you're impressed. Wimbledon's own walls, along nearly every significant corridor and passage, are lined with posters and signs featuring shots of past champions, lists

---

themselves are often traveling at over 90 mph, which is the speed of a big-league fastball. If you get down close enough to a pro court, you can hear an actual *sound* coming off the ball in flight, a kind of liquid hiss, from the combination of pace and spin. Close up and live, you'll also understand better the "open stance" that's become such an emblem of the power-baseline game. The term, after all, just means not turning one's side all the way to the net before hitting a groundstroke, and one reason why so many power-baseliners hit from the open stance is that the ball now is coming too fast for them to get turned all the way.

of Wimbledon facts and trivia, historic lore, and so on. Some of this stuff is interesting; some is just odd. The Wimbledon Lawn Tennis Museum, for instance, has a collection of all the various kinds of rackets used here through the decades, and one of the many signs along the Level 2 passage of the Millennium Building[5] promotes this exhibit with both photos and didactic text, a kind of History of the Racket. Here, *sic*, is the climactic end of this text:

> Today's lightweight frames made of space-age materials like graphite, boron, titanium and ceramics, with larger heads—mid-size (90–95 square inches) and over-size (110 square inches)—have totally transformed the character of the game. Nowadays it is the powerful hitters who dominate with heavy topspin. Serve-and-volley players and those who rely on subtlety and touch have virtually disappeared.

It seems odd, to say the least, that such a diagnosis continues to hang here so prominently in the fourth year of Federer's reign over Wimbledon, since the Swiss has brought to men's tennis degrees of touch and subtlety unseen since (at least) the days of McEnroe's prime. But the sign's really just a testament to the power of dogma. For almost two decades, the party line's been that certain advances in racket technology, conditioning, and weight training have transformed pro tennis from a game of quickness and finesse into one of athleticism and brute power. And, as an etiology of today's power-baseline game, this party line is broadly accurate. Today's pros truly are measurably bigger, stronger, and better conditioned,[6] and high-tech composite rackets really have increased their capacities for pace and spin. How, then, someone of Roger Federer's consummate

---

5. This is the large (and presumably six-year-old) structure where Wimbledon's administration, players, and media all have their respective areas and HQs.

6. (Some, like Nadal or Serena Williams, look more like cartoon superheroes than people.)

finesse has come to dominate the men's tour is a source of wide and dogmatic confusion.

There are three kinds of valid explanation for Federer's ascendancy. One kind involves mystery and metaphysics and is, I think, closest to the real truth. The others are more technical and make for better journalism.

The metaphysical explanation is that Roger Federer is one of those rare, preternatural athletes who appear to be exempt, at least in part, from certain physical laws. Good analogs here include Michael Jordan,[7] who could not only jump inhumanly high but actually hang there a beat or two longer than gravity allows, and Muhammad Ali, who really could "float" across the canvas and land two or three jabs in the clock-time required for one. There are probably a half-dozen other examples since 1960. And Roger Federer is of this type—a type that one could call genius, or mutant, or avatar. He is never hurried or off-balance. The approaching ball hangs, for

7. When asked, during the aforementioned Special One-on-One Interview, for examples of other athletes whose performances might seem beautiful to him, Federer mentions Jordan first, then Kobe Bryant, then "a soccer player like—guys who play very relaxed, like a Zinédine Zidane or something: he does great effort, but he seems like he doesn't need to try hard to get the results."

Federer's response to the subsequent question, which is what-all he makes of it when pundits and other players describe his own game as "beautiful," is interesting mainly because the response is pleasant, intelligent, and cooperative—as is Federer himself—without ever really saying anything (because, in fairness, what could one say about others' descriptions of him as beautiful? What would you say? It's ultimately a stupid question):

"It's always what people see first—for them, that's what you are 'best at.' When you used to watch John McEnroe, you know, the first time, what would you see? You would see a guy with incredible talent, because the way he played, nobody played like this. The way he played the ball, it was just all about *feel*. And then you go over to Boris Becker, and right away you saw a *powerful* player, you know?* When you see me play, you see a 'beautiful' player—and maybe after that you maybe see that he's fast, maybe you see that he's got a good forehand, maybe then you see that he has a good serve. First, you know, you have a base, and to me, I think it's great, you know, and I'm very lucky to be called basically 'beautiful,' you know, for style of play. Other ones have the 'grinder' [quality] first, [some] other ones are the 'power player,' [still] other ones are 'the quick guy.' With me it's, like, 'the beautiful player,' and that's really cool."

*(NB. Federer's big conversational tics are "maybe" and "you know." Ultimately, these tics are helpful because they serve as reminders of how appallingly young

him, a split-second longer than it ought to. His movements are lithe rather than athletic. Like Ali, Jordan, Maradona, and Gretzky, he seems both less and more substantial than the men he faces. Particularly in the all-white that Wimbledon enjoys getting away with still requiring, he looks like what he may well (I think) be: a creature whose body is both flesh and, somehow, light.

This thing about the ball cooperatively hanging there, slowing down, as if susceptible to the Swiss's will—there's real metaphysical truth here. And in the following anecdote. After a July 7 semifinal in which Federer destroyed Jonas Björkman—not just beat him, *destroyed* him—and just before a requisite post-match news conference in which Björkman, who's friendly with Federer, says he was pleased to "have the best seat in the house" to watch the Swiss "play the nearest to perfection you can play tennis," Federer and Björkman are evidently chatting and joking around, and Björkman asks him just how unnaturally big the ball was looking to him out there, and Federer confirms that it was "like a bowling ball or basketball." He means it just as a bantery, modest way to make Björkman feel better, to confirm that he's surprised by how unusually well he played today; but he's also revealing something about what tennis is like for him. Imagine that you're a person with preternaturally good reflexes and coordination and speed, and that you're playing high-level tennis. Your experience, in play, will not be that you possess phenomenal reflexes and speed; rather, it will seem to you that the tennis ball is quite large and slow-moving, and that you always have plenty of time to hit it. That is, you won't experience anything like the (empirically real) quickness and skill

---

he really is. If you're interested, the world's best tennis player is wearing white warm-up pants and a long-sleeved white microfiber shirt, possibly Nike. No sport coat, though. His handshake is only moderately firm, though the hand itself is like a carpentry rasp [for obvious reasons, tennis players tend to be very callusy]. He's a bit bigger than TV makes him seem—broader-shouldered, deeper in the chest. He's next to a table that's covered with visors and headbands, which he's been autographing with a Sharpie. He sits with his legs crossed and smiles pleasantly and seems very relaxed; he never fidgets with the Sharpie. One's overall impression is that Roger Federer is either a very nice guy or a guy who's very good at dealing with the media—or [most likely] both.)

that the live audience, watching tennis balls move so fast they hiss and blur, will attribute to you.[8]

Velocity's just one part of it. Now we're getting technical. Tennis is often called a game of inches, but the cliché is mostly referring to where a shot lands. In terms of a player's hitting an incoming ball, tennis is actually more a game of micrometers: vanishingly tiny changes around the moment of impact will have large effects on how and where the ball travels. The same principle explains why even the smallest imprecision in aiming a rifle will still cause a miss if the target's far enough away.

By way of illustration, let's slow things way down. Imagine that you, a tennis player, are standing just behind your deuce corner's baseline. A ball is served to your forehand—you pivot (or rotate) so that your side is to the ball's incoming path and start to take your racket back for the forehand return. Keep visualizing up to where you're about halfway into the stroke's forward motion; the incoming ball is now just off your front hip, maybe six inches from point of impact. Consider some of the variables involved here. On the vertical plane, angling your racket face just a couple degrees forward or back will create topspin or slice, respectively; keeping it perpendicular will produce a flat, spinless drive. Horizontally, adjusting the racket face ever so slightly to the left or right, and hitting the ball maybe a millisecond early or late, will result in a crosscourt versus down-the-line return. Further slight changes in the curves of your groundstroke's motion and follow-through will

8. Special One-on-One support from the man himself for this claim: "It's interesting, because this week, actually, Ancic [comma Mario, the towering top-ten Croatian whom Federer beat in Wednesday's quarterfinal] played on Centre Court against my friend, you know, the Swiss player Wawrinka [comma Stanislas, Federer's Davis Cup teammate], and I went to see it out where, you know, my girlfriend Mirka [Vavrinec, a former top-100 female player, knocked out by injury, who now basically functions as Federer's Alice B. Toklas] usually sits, and I went to see—for the first time since I have come here to Wimbledon, I went to see a match on Centre Court, and I was also surprised, actually, how fast, you know, the serve is and how fast you have to react to be able to get the ball back, especially when a guy like Mario [Ancic, who's known for his vicious serve] serves, you know? But then once you're on the court yourself, it's totally different, you know, because all you see is the ball, really, and you don't see the speed of the ball. . . ."

help determine how high your return passes over the net, which, together with the speed at which you're swinging (along with certain characteristics of the spin you impart), will affect how deep or shallow in the opponent's court your return lands, how high it bounces, etc. These are just the broadest distinctions, of course—like, there's heavy topspin vs. light topspin, sharply crosscourt vs. only slightly crosscourt, etc. There are also the issues of how close you're allowing the ball to get to your body, what grip you're using, the extent to which your knees are bent and/or weight's moving forward, and whether you're able simultaneously to watch the ball and to see what your opponent's doing after he serves. These all matter, too. Plus there's the fact that you're not putting a static object into motion here but rather reversing the flight and (to a varying extent) spin of a projectile coming toward you—coming, in the case of pro tennis, at speeds that make conscious thought impossible. Mario Ancic's first serve, for instance, often comes in around 130 mph. Since it's seventy-eight feet from Ancic's baseline to yours, that means it takes 0.41 seconds for his serve to reach you.[9] This is less than the time it takes to blink quickly, twice.

The upshot is that pro tennis involves intervals of time too brief for deliberate action. Temporally, we're more in the operative range of reflexes, purely physical reactions that bypass conscious thought. And yet an effective return of serve depends on a large set of decisions and physical adjustments that are a whole lot more involved and intentional than blinking, jumping when startled, etc.

Successfully returning a hard-served tennis ball requires what's sometimes called "the kinesthetic sense," meaning the ability to control the body and its artificial extensions through complex and

---

9. We're doing the math here with the ball traveling as the crow flies, for simplicity. Please do not write in with corrections. If you want to factor in the serve's bounce and so compute the total distance traveled by the ball as the sum of an oblique triangle's* two shorter legs, then by all means go ahead—you'll end up with between two and five additional hundredths of a second, which is not significant.

*(The slower a tennis court's surface, the closer to a right triangle you're going to have. On fast grass, the bounce's angle is always oblique.)

very quick systems of tasks. English has a whole cloud of terms for various parts of this ability: feel, touch, form, proprioception, coordination, hand-eye coordination, kinesthesia, grace, control, reflexes, and so on. For promising junior players, refining the kinesthetic sense is the main goal of the extreme daily practice regimens we often hear about.[10] The training here is both muscular and neurological. Hitting thousands of strokes, day after day, develops the ability to do by "feel" what cannot be done by regular conscious thought. Repetitive practice like this often looks tedious or even cruel to an outsider, but the outsider can't feel what's going on inside the player—tiny adjustments, over and over, and a sense of each change's effects that gets more and more acute even as it recedes from normal consciousness.[11]

The time and discipline required for serious kinesthetic training are one reason why top pros are usually people who've devoted most of their waking lives to tennis, starting (at the very latest) in their early teens. It was, for example, at age thirteen that Roger Federer finally gave up soccer, and a recognizable childhood, and entered Switzerland's national tennis training center in Ecublens. At sixteen, he dropped out of classroom studies and started serious international competition.

It was only weeks after quitting school that Federer won Junior Wimbledon. Obviously, this is something that not every junior who devotes himself to tennis can do. Just as obviously, then, there is more than time and training involved—there is also sheer talent, and degrees of it. Extraordinary kinesthetic ability must be present (and measurable) in a kid just to make the years of practice and training worthwhile . . . but from there, over time, the cream

---

10. Conditioning is also important, but this is mainly because the first thing that physical fatigue attacks is the kinesthetic sense. (Other antagonists are fear, self-consciousness, and extreme upset—which is why fragile psyches are rare in pro tennis.)

11. The best lay analogy is probably to the way an experienced driver can make all of good driving's myriad little decisions and adjustments without having to pay real attention to them.

starts to rise and separate. So one type of technical explanation for Federer's dominion is that he's just a bit more kinesthetically talented than the other male pros. Only a little bit, since everyone in the top 100 is himself kinesthetically gifted—but, then, tennis is a game of inches.

This answer is plausible but incomplete. It would probably not have been incomplete in 1980. In 2006, though, it's fair to ask why this kind of talent still matters so much. Recall what is true about dogma and Wimbledon's sign. Kinesthetic virtuoso or no, Roger Federer is now dominating the largest, strongest, fittest, best-trained and -coached field of male pros who've ever existed, with everyone using a kind of nuclear racket that's said to have made the finer calibrations of kinesthetic sense irrelevant, like trying to whistle Mozart during a Metallica concert.

According to reliable sources, honorary coin-tosser William Caines's backstory is that one day, when he was two and a half, his mother found a lump in his tummy, and took him to the doctor, and the lump was diagnosed as a malignant liver tumor. At which point one cannot, of course, imagine . . . a tiny child undergoing chemo, serious chemo, his mother having to watch, carry him home, nurse him, then bring him back to that place for more chemo. How did she answer her child's question—the big one, the obvious one? And who could answer hers? What could any priest or pastor say that wouldn't be grotesque?

It's 2–1 Nadal in the final's second set, and he's serving. Federer won the first set at love but then flagged a bit, as he sometimes does, and is quickly down a break. Now, on Nadal's ad, there's a sixteen-stroke point. Nadal is serving twenty mph faster than he did in Paris, and this one's down the center. Federer floats a soft forehand high over the net, which he can get away with because Nadal never comes in behind his serve. The Spaniard now hits a characteristically heavy topspin forehand deep to Federer's backhand; Federer comes back with an even heavier topspin backhand, almost a clay-court shot.

It's unexpected and backs Nadal up, slightly, and his response is a low hard short ball that lands just past the service line's T on Federer's forehand side. Against most other opponents, Federer could simply end the point on a ball like this, but one reason Nadal gives him trouble is that he's faster than the others, can get to stuff they can't; and so Federer here just hits a flat, medium-hard crosscourt forehand, going not for a winner but for a low, shallowly angled ball that forces Nadal up and out to the deuce side, his backhand. Nadal, on the run, backhands it hard down the line to Federer's backhand; Federer slices it right back down the same line, slow and floaty with backspin, making Nadal return to the same spot. Nadal slices the ball right back—three shots now all down the same line—and Federer slices the ball to the same spot yet again, this one even slower and floatier, and Nadal gets planted and hits a big two-hander down the same line—it's like Nadal's camped out now on his deuce side; he's no longer moving all the way back to the baseline's center between shots; Federer's hypnotized him a little. Federer now hits a very hard, deep topspin backhand, the kind that hisses, to a point just slightly on the ad side of Nadal's baseline, which Nadal gets to and forehands crosscourt; and Federer responds with an even harder, heavier crosscourt backhand, baseline-deep and moving so fast that Nadal has to hit the forehand off his back foot and then scramble to get to center as the shot lands maybe two feet short on Federer's backhand side again. Roger Federer steps to this ball and now hits a totally different crosscourt backhand, this one much shorter and sharper-angled, an angle no one would anticipate, and so heavy and blurred with topspin that it lands shallow and just inside the sideline and takes off hard after the bounce, and Nadal can't move in to cut it off and can't get to it laterally along the baseline, because of all the angle and topspin—end of point. It's a spectacular winner, a Federer Moment; but, watching it live, you can see that it's also a winner that Federer started setting up four or even five shots earlier. Everything after that first down-the-line slice was designed by the Swiss to maneuver Nadal and lull him and disrupt his rhythm and balance and open up that last, unimaginable angle—an angle that would have been impossible without extreme topspin.

Extreme topspin is the hallmark of today's power-baseline game. This is something that Wimbledon's sign gets right.[12] Why topspin is so key, though, is not commonly understood. What's commonly understood is that high-tech composite rackets impart much more pace to the ball, rather like aluminum baseball bats as opposed to good old lumber. But that dogma is false. The truth is that, at the same tensile strength, carbon-based composites are lighter than wood, and this allows modern rackets to be a couple ounces lighter and at least an inch wider across the face than the vintage Kramer and Maxply. It's the width of the face that's vital. A wider face means there's more total string area, which means the sweet spot's bigger. With a composite racket, you don't have to meet the ball in the precise geometric center of the strings in order to generate good pace. Nor must you be spot-on to generate topspin, a spin that (recall) requires a tilted face and upwardly curved stroke, brushing over the ball rather than hitting flat through it—this was quite hard to do with wood rackets, because of their smaller face and niggardly sweet spot. Composites' lighter, wider heads and more generous centers let players swing faster and put way more topspin on the ball . . . and, in turn, the more topspin you put on the ball, the harder you can hit it, because there's more margin for error. Topspin causes the ball to pass high over the net, describe a sharp arc, and come down fast into the opponent's court (instead of maybe soaring out).

So the basic formula here is that composite rackets enable topspin, which in turn enables groundstrokes vastly faster and harder than twenty years ago—it's common now to see male pros pulled up off the ground and halfway around in the air by the force of

12. (. . . assuming, that is, that the sign's "with heavy topspin" is modifying "dominate" rather than "powerful hitters," which actually it might or might not—British grammar is a bit dodgy)

their strokes, which in the old days was something one saw only in Jimmy Connors.

Connors was not, by the way, the father of the power-baseline game. He whaled mightily from the baseline, true, but his ground-strokes were flat and spinless and had to pass very low over the net. Nor was Björn Borg a true power-baseliner. Both Borg and Connors played specialized versions of the classic baseline game, which had evolved as a counterforce to the even more classic serve-and-volley game, which was itself the dominant form of men's power tennis for decades, and of which John McEnroe was the greatest modern exponent. You probably know all this, and may also know that McEnroe toppled Borg and then more or less ruled the men's game until the appearance, around the early mid-1980s, of (a) modern composite rackets[13] and (b) Ivan Lendl, who played with an early form of composite and was the true progenitor of power-baseline tennis.[14]

Ivan Lendl was the first top pro whose strokes and tactics appeared to be designed around the special capacities of the composite racket. His goal was to win points from the baseline, via either passing shots or outright winners. His weapon was his groundstrokes, especially his forehand, which he could hit with overwhelming pace because of the amount of topspin he put on the ball. The blend of pace and topspin also allowed Lendl to do something that proved crucial to the advent of the power-baseline game. He could pull off radical, extraordinary angles on hard-hit groundstrokes, mainly because of the speed with which heavy top-spin makes the ball dip and land without going wide. In retrospect, this changed the whole physics of aggressive tennis. For decades,

---

13. (which neither Connors nor McEnroe could switch to with much success—their games were fixed around pre-modern rackets)

14. Form-wise, with his whippy forehand, lethal one-hander, and merciless treatment of short balls, Lendl somewhat anticipated Federer. But the Czech was also stiff, cold, and brutal; his game was awesome but not beautiful. (My college doubles partner used to describe watching Lendl as like getting to see *Triumph of the Will* in 3-D.)

it had been angle that made the serve-and-volley game so lethal. The closer one is to the net, the more of the opponent's court is open—the classic advantage of volleying was that you could hit angles that would go way wide if attempted from the baseline or midcourt. But topspin on a groundstroke, if it's really extreme, can bring the ball down fast and shallow enough to exploit many of these same angles. Especially if the groundstroke you're hitting is off a somewhat short ball—the shorter the ball, the more angles are possible. Pace, topspin, and aggressive baseline angles: and lo, it's the power-baseline game.

It wasn't that Ivan Lendl was an immortally great tennis player. He was simply the first top pro to demonstrate what heavy topspin and raw power could achieve from the baseline. And, most important, the achievement was replicable, just like the composite racket. Past a certain threshold of physical talent and training, the main requirements were athleticism, aggression, and superior strength and conditioning. The result (omitting various complications and subspecialties[15]) has been men's pro tennis for the last twenty years: ever bigger, stronger, fitter players generating unprecedented pace and topspin off the ground, trying to force the short or weak ball that they can put away.

Illustrative stat: When Lleyton Hewitt defeated David Nalbandian in the 2002 Wimbledon men's final, there was not one single serve-and-volley point.[16]

The generic power-baseline game is not boring—certainly not compared with the two-second points of old-time serve-and-volley or the moonball tedium of classic baseline attrition. But it is somewhat static and limited; it is not, as pundits have publicly feared for years, the evolutionary endpoint of tennis. The player who's shown this to be true is Roger Federer. And he's shown it from *within* the modern game.

15. See, for one example, the continued effectiveness of some serve-and-volley (mainly in the adapted, heavily ace- and quickness-dependent form of a Sampras or Rafter) on fast courts through the 1990s.

16. It's also illustrative that 2002 was Wimbledon's last pre-Federer final.

This *within* is what's important here; this is what a purely neu-ral account leaves out. And it is why sexy attributions like touch and subtlety must not be misunderstood. With Federer, it's not either/or. The Swiss has every bit of Lendl's and Agassi's pace on his groundstrokes, and leaves the ground when he swings, and can out-hit even Nadal from the backcourt.[17] What's strange and wrong about Wimbledon's sign, really, is its overall dolorous tone. Sub-tlety, touch, and finesse are not dead in the power-baseline era. For it is, still, in 2006, very much the power-baseline era: Roger Federer is a first-rate, kick-ass power-baseliner. It's just that that's not all he is. There's also his intelligence, his occult anticipation, his court sense, his ability to read and manipulate opponents, to mix spins and speeds, to misdirect and disguise, to use tactical foresight and peripheral vision and kinesthetic range instead of just rote pace—

17. In the '06 final's third set, at three games all and 30–15, Nadal kicks his second serve high to Federer's backhand. Nadal's clearly been coached to go high and heavy to Federer's backhand, and that's what he does, point after point. Federer slices the return back to Nadal's center and two feet short—not short enough to let the Spaniard hit a winner, but short enough to draw him slightly into the court, whence Nadal winds up and puts all his forehand's strength into a hard heavy shot to (again) Federer's backhand. The pace he's put on the ball means that Nadal is still back-pedaling to his baseline as Federer leaves his feet and cranks a very hard topspin backhand down the line to Nadal's deuce side, which Nadal—out of position but world-class fast—reaches and manages to one-hand back deep to (again) Federer's backhand side, but this ball's floaty and slow, and Federer has time to step around and hit an inside-out forehand, a forehand as hard as anyone's hit all tournament, with just enough topspin to bring it down in Nadal's ad corner, and the Spaniard gets there but can't return it. Big ovation. Again, what looks like an overwhelming baseline winner was actually set up by that first clever semi-short slice and Nadal's own predictability about where and how hard he'll hit every ball. Federer surely whaled that last forehand, though. People are looking at each other and applauding. The thing with Federer is that he's Mozart and Metallica at the same time, and the harmony's somehow exquisite.

By the way, it's right around here, or the next game, watching, that three sepa-rate inner-type things come together and mesh. One is a feeling of deep personal privilege at being alive to get to see this; another is the thought that William Caines is probably somewhere here in the Centre Court crowd, too, watching, maybe with his mum. The third thing is a sudden memory of the earnest way the press bus driver promised just this experience. Because there is one. It's hard to describe—it's like a thought that's also a feeling. One wouldn't want to make too much of it, or to pretend that it's any sort of equitable balance; that would be grotesque. But the truth is that whatever deity, entity, energy, or random genetic flux produces sick children also produced Roger Federer, and just look at him down there. Look at that.

all this has exposed the limits, and possibilities, of men's tennis as it's now played.

. . . Which sounds very high-flown and nice, of course, but please understand that with this guy it's not high-flown or abstract. Or nice. In the same emphatic, empirical, dominating way that Lendl drove home his own lesson, Roger Federer is showing that the speed and strength of today's pro game are merely its skeleton, not its flesh. He has, figuratively and literally, re-embodied men's tennis, and for the first time in years the game's future is unpredictable. You should have seen, on the grounds' outside courts, the variegated ballet that was this year's Junior Wimbledon. Drop volleys and mixed spins, off-speed serves, gambits planned three shots ahead—all as well as the standard-issue grunts and booming balls. Whether anything like a nascent Federer was here among these juniors can't be known, of course. Genius is not replicable. Inspiration, though, is contagious, and multiform—and even just to see, close up, power and aggression made vulnerable to beauty is to feel inspired and (in a fleeting, mortal way) reconciled.

2006

Sources and Acknowledgments

Derivative Sport in Tornado Alley first appeared, as "Tennis, Trigonometry, Tornadoes: A Midwestern Boyhood," in *Harper's Magazine*, December 1991. The text used here is from *A Supposedly Fun Thing I'll Never Do Again*, by David Foster Wallace (Little, Brown and Company, 1997). Copyright © 1997 by David Foster Wallace.

How Tracy Austin Broke My Heart first appeared, as "Tracy Austin Serves Up a Bubbly Life Story," in *The Philadelphia Inquirer*, August 30, 1992. The text used here is from *Consider the Lobster and Other Essays*, by David Foster Wallace (Little, Brown and Company, 2006). Copyright © 2006 by David Foster Wallace.

Tennis Player Michael Joyce's Professional Artistry as a Paradigm of Certain Stuff about Choice, Freedom, Limitation, Joy, Grotesquerie, and Human Completeness first appeared, as "The String Theory," in *Esquire*, July 1996. The text used here is from *A Supposedly Fun Thing I'll Never Do Again*, by David Foster Wallace (Little, Brown and Company, 1997). Copyright © 1997 by David Foster Wallace.

Democracy and Commerce at the U.S. Open first appeared in *Tennis*, September 1996. The text used here is from *Both Flesh and Not*, by David Foster Wallace (Little, Brown and Company, 2012). Copyright © 2012 by David Foster Wallace Literary Trust.

Federer Both Flesh and Not first appeared, as "Federer as Religious Experience," in *The New York Times PLAY Magazine*, August 20, 2006. The text used here is from *Both Flesh and Not*, by David Foster Wallace (Little, Brown and Company, 2012). Copyright © 2012 by David Foster Wallace Literary Trust.

About the Author

DAVID FOSTER WALLACE was born in Ithaca, New York, in 1962, and was raised in Illinois. He received bachelor of arts degrees in English and philosophy from Amherst College and a master of fine arts degree from the University of Arizona. His first novel, *The Broom of the System*, was published in 1987, and his second, *Infinite Jest*, in 1996. He also published three short-story collections, two essay collections, a book about hip-hop (written with his friend Mark Costello), and a brief history of infinity. He was the recipient of a MacArthur Fellowship, a Whiting Writers' Award, and a Lannan Literary Award, and was a member of the usage panel for *The American Heritage Dictionary of the English Language.* He died in 2008. His novel *The Pale King* and his essay collection *Both Flesh and Not* were published posthumously.

About John Jeremiah Sullivan

JOHN JEREMIAH SULLIVAN was born in Louisville, Kentucky, in 1974. A staff writer for *The New York Times Magazine* and the Southern editor of *The Paris Review*, he is the recipient of two National Magazine Awards, a Whiting Award, a Pushcart Prize, and a Windham-Campbell Literature Prize. He is the author of three books, *Blood Horses* (2004), *Pulphead* (2011), and the forthcoming *Prime Minister of Paradise* (2017), and the editor of *The Best American Essays 2014*. He lives in North Carolina with his wife and daughters.

This book is set in Warnock Pro Light, a font designed
by Adobe senior type designer Robert Slimbach.
It is named after Adobe's cofounder John Warnock.

The paper is acid-free Sebago Antique, manufactured by
the Lindenmeyr Paper Company. The binding material is
Rainbow Emerald with BB embossing, on which the type
has been debossed and stamped with pigment foil.

Printing and binding by R. R. Donnelley, Crawfordsville, Indiana.
Text design and composition by Gopa & Ted2, Inc.
Cover and endpaper design by Pete Garceau.